REAWAKENING

REAWAKENING

*Return of Lightness and Peace
after My Daughter's Murder*

BARBARA A. MANGI

MOUNTAIN ARBOR PRESS

MOUNTAIN ARBOR
   PRESS
Alpharetta, GA

The author has tried to recreate events, locations, and conversations from his/her memories of them. In some instances, in order to maintain their anonymity, the author has changed the names of individuals and places. He/she may also have changed some identifying characteristics and details such as physical attributes, occupations, and places of residence.

To preserve the integrity of the original documents, all journal entries, court transcriptions, and letters have been left unedited, except for minor formatting adjustments as needed for ease of reading.

Copyright © 2017 by Barbara A. Mangi

All rights reserved. No part of this book may be reproduced or transmitted in any form or by any means, electronic or mechanical, including photocopying, recording, or any information storage and retrieval system, without permission in writing from the author.

ISBN: 978-1-63183-170-6

Library of Congress Control Number: 2017913675

10 9 8 7 6 5 4 3 2   0 9 2 1 1 7

Printed in the United States of America

∞This paper meets the requirements of ANSI/NISO Z39.48-1992 (Permanence of Paper)

Scripture texts, prefaces, introductions, footnotes, and crossreferences used in this work are taken from the New American Bible, revised edition © 2010, 1991, 1986, 1970 Confraternity of Christian Doctrine, Inc., Washington, DC. All rights reserved. No part of this work may be reproduced or transmitted in any form or by any means, electronic or mechanical, including photocopying, recording, or by any information storage and retrieval system, without permission in writing from the copyright owner.

I dedicate this book to:

My husband, Joe, who has walked my life journey with me for forty-two years, who gave me two most cherished daughters, and whose love I never doubted even when, at times, I may not have been easy to love.

My daughters, to whom I gave life and joyfully welcomed into my heart and my world. I will forever cherish all of our memories.

My firstborn daughter, Sarah, whose most treasured gift of unconditional love is always freely given to me, and who fills me with great pride and joy as I look forward with excitement to sharing her life journey for years to come.

And in loving memory to my younger daughter, Dana, whose beautiful spirit will forever shine brightly within my heart, and who continues to make a difference in this world through all of us who love her.

*I have been through a lot and have suffered a great deal.
But I have had lots of happy moments as well. Every
moment one lives is different from the other.
The good, the bad, hardship, the joy, the tragedy, love, and
happiness are all interwoven into one single, indescribable
whole that is called life.
You cannot separate the good from the bad. And perhaps
there is no need to do so, either.*

—Jacqueline Kennedy Onassis

CONTENTS

Introduction xi

Chapter 1: Nothing Seemed Out of the Ordinary 1

Chapter 2: Trying to Keep It Together 7

Chapter 3: Observations 11

Chapter 4: Our World Comes Crashing Down 13

Chapter 5: Seeing the Face of God 19

Chapter 6: The First Night 23

Chapter 7: Taking Care of Business 25

Chapter 8: Heart Wrenching yet Comforting 35

Chapter 9: The Aftermath 45

Chapter 10: Really, God? 49

Chapter 11: One Day at a Time 53

Chapter 12: Salt in the Wound 61

Chapter 13: Now What Do I Do? 69

Chapter 14: The First Holidays Loom 75

Chapter 15: A New Year Dawns 81

Chapter 16: Life Goes On 87

Chapter 17: Tangled Web of Emotions — 93

Chapter 18: Never in My Wildest Dreams — 97

Chapter 19: First Anniversary of Dana's Death — 101

Chapter 20: A Better Place — 109

Chapter 21: The Excruciatingly Slow Court Process — 113

Chapter 22: Trial or No Trial? — 119

Chapter 23: An Emotional Shift — 123

Chapter 24: Heightened Anticipation — 125

Chapter 25: March 11, 2010 — 129

Chapter 26: Life Changer — 143

Chapter 27: Where Do I Go from Here? — 149

Chapter 28: Retreats — 153

Chapter 29: A New Struggle — 157

Chapter 30: Developing a Spiritual Connection — 165

Chapter 31: My Personal and Unique Relationship with God — 191

Chapter 32: Coming Full Circle — 195

Acknowledgments — 209
Additional Resources — 211
Bibliography — 217

INTRODUCTION

On the early morning of August 19, 2007, my most feared nightmare and my hell on earth began when my husband and I received a phone call telling us our younger daughter, Dana, had been brutally murdered in Chicago the night before. No words seem adequate to describe how this affected me. In the deepest level of my being, I was like a wounded animal with an immeasurable, unrelenting pain, as if a part of my heart had been ripped out. On another level, I was filled with such a heart-wrenching sadness for my older daughter, Sarah. In losing her sister and her only sibling, her life had been shattered and her dreams forever altered. Losing my own child is the worst pain I think I will ever endure. A piece of me was torn away that day. But somehow I just existed, and exist was all I did for some time.

I was and still am a strong woman and a fighter. This time I was in for the most demanding and challenging fight of my life. A part of me died that Sunday morning. I had tragically lost my mother when I was young, and my dad just six weeks before Dana's murder. As painful and sad as those two losses were, they did not even come close to the emptiness and overwhelming anguish I experienced after losing my child. I dug deep and tapped into the strength I had developed from my life experiences, good and bad, to survive this indescribable tragedy. I used that strength and courage to fight through this hellish nightmare. Sadly, I was a daughter who had lost her mother at a young age and was a mother who had now lost her daughter at a young age.

How does anyone survive something as unthinkable, shocking, devastating, and horrific as the murder of their child? To this day, over nine years later, people still cannot imagine us getting back to a normal life and finding pleasure in that. I might have wondered the same thing before this happened to us. Each person must find his or her own way of dealing with such a loss, to find whatever resources will give them comfort, support, and healing in their overwhelming grief and sorrow. I believe that, sadly, some people never find their way through their grief and heartache to recover and heal. They remain in their recurring nightmare for the rest of their lives.

Within six months of Dana's death, I began to feel a strong desire to help others through their grief. Back then, I had no idea of how I would act on that desire to help others. I never imagined that would entail writing a book. But as I journeyed along my own grieving and healing path during the next four to five years, I wanted to share my story. Although the pain of losing Dana will never completely disappear, I learned to cope and to keep living despite tragedy. Through those years, I was often in awe of where I was, of how I had gotten there, of the mystery and miracle of it all, and of how I fought to climb from the deepest depths of despair to peace and healing. How did that happen? Early in my grieving process, I would never have believed I would or could get to this place of peace again. If that could happen to me, then by sharing my story, I might help others whose loved ones have been murdered.

The passing of time, my strong faith, the love and support of our entire family and our amazing friends, and the choices I made along the way that helped me heal led me toward a light in the distance. This journey was filled with quite a few roadblocks along the way, some that were out of my control and others over which I had some control. Thinking back on that dark period over nine years ago, I am most proud that I persevered in staying true to myself. I believe God has nudged and guided me through my hell on earth to lead me where I am today.

This is my story. It is a story of survival, of self-discovery, of pain and suffering, of perseverance and strength, of strong faith in God and the hope of being reunited with my daughter again, of the healing power of forgiveness, of the wonder and mystery in how I felt lightness and peace return to my soul. My story is unique because of my own personal struggles, faults and weaknesses, strengths, losses, joys, and blessings, with many moments of happiness. Of course, my life story did not start on that fateful morning in August 2007. I have been broken many times throughout my life, but I survived and have become even stronger and more focused. All that I was before that horrifying day and all that I am today is a rich tapestry of *my* life experiences, each of which has influenced who I am and all that I have done.

I never had a plan for surviving Dana's murder, nor for navigating this unthinkable journey as a mother who had lost her child. Never would I have imagined how much I would learn about myself and about my faith. My heart aches for anyone who has lost a loved one to murder and for any parent who has felt the heart-wrenching pain of losing a child. I hope this book can be a help, a guide for other people who have lost someone to murder to find healing in their own way. I do not know which path is the one you should follow. Instead, my heart yearns to share the life-giving lessons I learned along the way. In sharing the story of my flawed and human journey, I pray that you may discover your own path, a path that leads you in your unique healing journey toward a place of lightness and peace. I pray that your heart may find joy and happiness in living life once again.

As you travel this unthinkable journey with me, may the life-giving lessons I learned give you the strength and courage to chart your own path toward healing.

CHAPTER 1

NOTHING SEEMED OUT OF THE ORDINARY

As 2007 began, I had so much to be thankful for. I was happy and content. I had been blessed with a good life and did not want for much. Joe and I were parents of two adult daughters, Sarah and Dana. We were thoroughly enjoying being empty nesters, and our daughters were coming into their own as young adults. I was confident in their abilities to define their own lives. We had raised these two beautiful, smart, responsible, caring, generous, spiritual, and loving young women. I had witnessed and supported them as they navigated their chosen paths. I could not wait to share their journeys in these next phases of their lives. Life was good.

As a family, the twenty-five years we had spent together were not perfect, but they were full of love and happiness. And there was never a dull moment in our lives! In July 2007, Dana was moving to Minneapolis, Minnesota, to begin veterinary school in late August. Dana's spirit had been crushed after being denied admittance the prior two years. This year she had realized her dream and was accepted into the University of Minnesota's College of Veterinary Medicine. Sarah, working full time at a Chicago bank as a financial analyst and attending evening classes at the University of Chicago, was set to graduate with a master of business administration (MBA) in August 2007. She had always thought she wanted to be a Wall Street trader. But, as graduation approached, Sarah became more confused about what she wanted to pursue. This dilemma was something new. Sarah had been quite focused and had her future planned for years. Unbeknownst to me, she was formulating another plan, to apply to law school at the University of Minnesota. If it all worked out as planned, she and Dana would be in Minneapolis together for several years!

I was in a good place with Joe in our marriage in 2007, although I had not always felt that way. I had grown up in an abusive, alcoholic family, witnessing my dad physically abusing my mom. No child should have to witness that—the emotional trauma, I believe, left my siblings and me scarred. Because of living in this dysfunctional family, I had assumed the unhealthy role of a caretaker of my younger siblings who were vulnerable and not old enough to fend for themselves. For many years, I had carried around emotional baggage from my past, including believing in that role as caretaker for everyone but me. I had brought that into my marriage. I excelled at taking care of my family, and my husband and daughters were the benefactors of my giving and nurturing nature, as unhealthy as that was for all of us. For many years, I had no idea I was in such an unhealthy place. I rarely asked for help from my husband, but continued like a madwoman. As a result, as we entered the 1990s, I was so exhausted I could not feel any emotions anymore. And, for the most part, I had been good at hiding my numbness from my loved ones. I did not realize being a caretaker was so detrimental to me, my relationship with my husband, and my daughters.

I didn't get help until I turned forty. A medical crisis, being diagnosed with an aggressive breast cancer that year, devastated me and was the catalyst that finally made me realize being a caretaker of everyone but myself had to stop! I no longer wanted to live like that. I began to see Rita, a psychotherapist, whom I would then continue to see off and on for the next sixteen years, both in individual and group therapy. Through hard work, Rita helped me to rediscover myself and find my voice in my relationships. As I worked on being more open and honest with my feelings, I struggled to get Joe to open up to me too. Now, in 2007, I continued my healing journey with Rita. Although I was not always content in my marriage—all marriages have their ups and downs, especially after thirty-two years of marriage—I had a husband who loved me and I hoped that, in our marriage, we would achieve a stronger and closer emotional bond.

In July 2007, Joe and I helped Dana move to Minneapolis, Minnesota. She returned home in early August for a two-week visit before starting her four-year vet school program. We had a wonderful family celebration for both Sarah and Dana graduating with master's degrees that summer and for Dana being accepted into veterinary school. While visiting, Dana was home during the days with Riley, our dog, and Moose, her dog, while Joe and I were at work. Somewhat bored since all her friends and her sister were working, she had asked me to take off work. Having recently started a new job, I was not going to ask for time off. But we did hang out together some evenings and went to see the Harry Potter movie, *Order of the Phoenix*, one night. The week flew by.

Friday night, Dana met friends for the evening. Although my individual counseling sessions were rare, I still participated in group therapy with Rita. I stayed overnight with Sarah at her condo downtown that night because I had a 9:00 a.m. group therapy session on Saturday morning at Rita's downtown Chicago office. Since Dana would not be home until late Friday evening and Joe was out of town until later Saturday night, it would be nice to spend an evening with Sarah and walk to Rita's office Saturday morning. I would see Dana when I got home that afternoon. Sometime later Friday evening, I texted Dana to see if she was home yet. She was still with her friends and would text me when she was back at our house. I got that message before I went to bed Friday night. When she stayed with us, Dana was always good about texting or calling if she would be out late.

My Saturday went as planned, for the most part. After our group therapy session ended at noon, I was on my way back to Sarah's place when Dana called me. She had spilled nail-polish remover on the family room table and taken the finish off a "large area." She could tell that I was aggravated, but I did not yell at her. Once I arrived at Sarah's place, I got my backpack, said goodbye to her, and headed back to the suburbs. Dana had called Sarah before she got up the nerve to call me and had told her, "Mom's going to kill me." Sarah and I laughed about that. I figured I would see Dana when I got home but made a couple of stops on my way.

As I was driving, I received a text message from Dana saying she knew I was mad. She wanted to tell me she was going to a party with Pat in Wrigleyville, around Wrigley Field in Chicago, to watch the Cubs game. I called her back and we talked about the spill on the table. I explained that I had almost done that same thing many times, too lazy to put a towel under my hand while polishing my nails. I had one request; I asked her to look up solutions for repairing the damage before she headed back to Minneapolis.

She wanted to know when I was coming home. When I told her I was making a few stops, she said she might be gone when I got back. I don't know why, but in that moment, I asked her if this was the "Pat" she had known from Loyola five to six years earlier, who had been a jerk to her. I knew no specifics, just general things she had shared with me all those years ago. Back then, I had been glad when he was out of her life. She said it was him but then changed the subject. At that point, I thought about telling her to be careful, but I kept my mouth shut. She was, after all, twenty-five years old and an adult who made her own decisions.

In any case, I felt uneasy because she was going to Wrigleyville alone, something I did not think she ever did. On my way home, I picked up something for dinner since neither Joe nor Dana would be home. I texted Dana to see if she wanted me to pick something up for her to eat later. She responded that they would probably eat near Wrigley Field at one of the bars. We had one more phone conversation when she called to tell me she had just left our house and would see me later. I told her to be careful driving home.

That was the last time I talked to my younger daughter.

When I returned home and saw the "large area" that had been damaged on our wood table, I chuckled. It was not large at all, and I was glad I had not overreacted to her news. Every time I dust that table, with a bittersweet smile, I remember Dana. I am thankful Dana's apology got more attention than the little spot that day.

Saturday evening I hung out at home, reading and watching TV, nothing out of the ordinary. It was a nasty, stormy evening causing rain delays at Wrigley Field. Joe arrived home late, was tired, and went to bed. When I was finally ready to go to bed about 12:30 a.m. Sunday morning, I texted Dana telling her I was going to bed, asking her where she was, and telling her again to be careful driving home. It was odd that she hadn't texted me. Usually, she would comment about the Cubs game or let me know if she was coming home later than expected. But I had gotten no response. I went to bed realizing it could be any number of reasons; her cell phone died or maybe it was in her purse in a corner somewhere, or she was having a great time and not checking her phone.

CHAPTER 2

TRYING TO KEEP IT TOGETHER

At about 1:30 a.m., I awoke because of a reaction to one of my medications. Dana was not home yet and I had received no text, so I went downstairs to read and called her cell phone. No answer. By now I could not go back to sleep, so I just lay on the couch trying to concentrate on my book. I think I called her and sent a text every hour after that for the next few hours with the same results.

I tried to remain calm, hoping there was an explanation. All this time Joe was sleeping and I did not want to alarm him yet. I was trying, in vain, to convince myself she may have drunk too much and was sleeping it off at this party—praying that wherever she was, she was safe. But other more unthinkable and unwelcome thoughts sabotaged my attempts to remain calm. Had she been attacked walking to her parked car after the party? I had horrible visions of her lying injured, or worse, somewhere on this miserable, stormy night. The weirdest thing is that I never once thought Dana might have been in a car accident on the way home. Was this my mother's intuition?

Why did I not wake my husband when I first woke up? I was convinced that as soon as I told Joe I was worried, he would react, and I was not ready yet to accept the worst-case scenario. I spent those long hours on the couch trying to remain calm and convince myself there must be a reasonable explanation for all of this. But in the early hours of that Sunday morning, I had never felt more alone. It is a memory I may never be able to erase, and it haunted me for a long time.

Please, please, please God, let my Dana be all right.

I know God is always with me, even though sometimes I do

not remember to talk to Him and ask for what I need. This night I could not think of asking God to comfort me; all I could do was plead for my daughter's safe return.

At about 4:00 a.m., I was frantic with worry and fear for my daughter. I texted Dana once more, saying I was worried and to please text me back. Still no answer. Just after that text, Joe woke up and came down to see where I was. I told him Dana was not home yet, that she had gone into the city for a party and that I was worried. He sprang into action. He wanted us to drive down to Wrigleyville and look for Dana's car. But we had no idea what this guy's last name was, where he lived, or his phone number. I debated calling Sarah to see if she knew Pat's last name or where he might live down in Wrigleyville, but I did not want to scare her. Even if she knew his last name, what good would that do? I cannot even begin to describe how helpless I felt. I talked Joe out of filing a missing-persons report, because Dana was with a friend and was twenty-five years old. Wouldn't the police ask us why we assumed she was missing after less than twelve hours? They didn't know what kind of young woman she was and that she always let us know when her plans changed. It seemed too early to call the police. Dana had a shower to attend that Sunday afternoon. I hoped she had just slept in Wrigleyville and would show up at home early that morning to rest a bit and get ready.

But at 5:00 a.m., Joe could not wait any longer and called the Belmont police station, the station closest to the Wrigleyville area, to see if a young woman had been taken to a hospital nearby. The officer said no but took Dana's name. An hour later Joe called again and the same officer answered the phone. Somewhat aggravated, he replied, "We have no reports of a young woman being brought to a hospital. If I were you and your wife, I would start thinking of a punishment for your daughter when she gets home!" Really? All I could think about was how rude and uncaring that statement was.

Finally, I told Joe I needed to get an hour of sleep after which I would get up and try her phone one more time. By then it would be about 7:00 a.m. If I got no answer, we would call the police once again. How could this be happening to us?

I couldn't fall asleep, but I got a brief rest and then called Dana's cell phone one more time, getting no answer. As I lay in bed, working up the courage to call the police again, the phone rang. Joe was downstairs and both he and I answered the phone at the same time. When I heard a man's voice, I hung up right away because I thought it was Joe's company calling about a charter flight for him. Then Joe walked into the bedroom, holding the phone to his ear, and said in a calm voice, "Dana is dead, she was murdered." He must have been in shock already. All I remember is my screaming and moaning. The lead detective apparently apologized to Joe for telling us over the phone. This story was already all over the news channels and they did not want us to hear it first by turning on the TV.

CHAPTER 3

OBSERVATIONS

From the moment I heard Joe's words, it was a struggle for me to get through every minute of every day for some time. But something kept me going. First and foremost, my faith carried me. I accepted fairly quickly that Dana was at peace and in heaven with her loving God and Father, where she would never be hurt again. However, I didn't agree with well-intentioned people who tried to comfort me by saying Dana was in a better place. These words irritated me, and I hated what I thought back then was God's plan. I was in so much pain, sorrow, and shock. And, although I was near emotional collapse and meltdown, I never gave up on my God. Nor did I pull away from the church. Of course, I did ask Him *why He had taken her from us*. But my God has always been a loving God, not a vengeful or punishing God, and so my most personal relationship with Him deepened as I prayed. And I prayed without ceasing.

I had a husband and another daughter who were also part of me. Almost immediately, my husband had shut down on me. My own emotional scars from childhood were deep seated, so when my husband shut me out of sharing his pain and sorrow, my childhood feelings of vulnerability, abandonment, and being left alone to deal with this trauma resurfaced. My emotional healing had already taken many years and was a work in progress. And yet, my biggest obstacles had always been in times of crisis when I experienced the most difficulty in remaining open and honest in my relationship with Joe. How were we going to survive this inconceivable tragedy? Our marriage and relationship would be tested in the months and years to come. Then there was Sarah, whom I love more than my own life; I could not give up and abandon her.

Was I conscious of these thoughts that Sunday morning? No! I was barely able to function, but somehow I managed. Being in shock saved me and got me through the first week or so.

CHAPTER 4

OUR WORLD COMES CRASHING DOWN

In that fleeting moment when Joe appeared in our bedroom doorway and said, "Dana is dead, she was murdered," my life was forever changed. Sometimes I still cannot wrap my mind around the reality of Dana's murder. Shock and numbness threatened to consume me that morning as I tried to comprehend the incomprehensible. From deep within, I felt the "Dana" part of my heart and soul being ripped from me as wailing and moaning spilled from my throat.

How could a person do this to another human being, especially to my beautiful Dana? Who? Why? How was this possible?

I do not know how anyone could function after hearing the unthinkable, horrific news we heard that morning. I can only surmise shock calmed me enough to question Joe about the phone conversation and then make decisions. Detective Ed, the lead detective, had broken the news to Joe and explained that usually the police came to the house to inform the family of the death of their loved one. In our case, they had been concerned we might be up already and would see Dana's murder story on TV, hence the phone call. He suggested we not turn on the TV. Since the reporters were not getting their facts from the police, the reports might not be accurate. Joe was also instructed not to come down to the crime scene or to the police department. I yearned to go to my baby girl and, just for a while, be with her. However, that was not an option and I did not have the energy to question their decision. Detective Ed would be in touch as soon as he could to give us more information. When Joe informed me the killer's name was Joe Ford, it did not ring a bell with me.

Thank God, at least it was not the Pat whom Dana met last night.

Before doing anything else, I rashly called Sarah; I did not want her to wake up and turn on the TV to this unimaginable, devastating news. Not that she ever got up that early on a Sunday, but I was not thinking clearly. How is it possible I have no vivid recollection of that conversation with Sarah? Numbed by the events as they had unfolded, I was unable to focus on anything or think through any decision. Therefore, it is not surprising that my memories of that phone call are hidden behind a dense fog. Sarah explained later that the first thing she heard was my crying, and she had sensed it was an agitated and painful cry. Since Joe is a pilot and had been on a trip the night before, she cried, "Did something happen to Dad? Is he okay?"

My sobbing and moaning worsened as I tried to tell her that Dana had been murdered. She could not understand me at first and continued asking me about Joe. Finally, she understood, and her painful realization led her to scream, "What happened, where was she, who did this to her? I want to go be with her."

"We don't know exactly what happened. Dad says the murderer's name is Joe Ford. I just know she was meeting Pat, a friend she knew from college, to go to a party down in Wrigleyville to watch the Cubs game. The police won't allow us to see her at the crime scene. Dad and I are driving down there to be with you. Can you call a friend to come stay with you until we arrive?"

I just want to be with my Sarah NOW, wrap her in my arms, protect her from this hellish nightmare, and never let her go. How will she survive this news? She is all alone down there! God, please keep her safe for us. We've got to get down there! Is this really happening? Should Joe and I even drive downtown? We are in no condition to do this, but I must get down there. I need to call Rita to tell her about Dana and just talk to her for a few minutes.

One of my most horrible memories of that morning and one of my biggest regrets is making that heartbreaking call to Sarah, alone in the city, to tell her that her sister and only sibling had been murdered. Even now, my heart aches knowing I inflicted unimaginable trauma on her and that she was alone until her friend, Chris, arrived to stay with and comfort her while we were on our way downtown.

Although I cannot recall any of my conversations or interactions that morning, I do know that one of my sisters-in-law came over and took charge of Riley and my phone list. With my other sister-in-law's help, the two of them notified family and friends. They were the first of our many angels on this perilous, life-changing journey. Unable to reach my therapist, Rita, I left her a voicemail asking her to call me as soon as possible. I do not even remember if I told her Dana had been murdered. Once all my calls were made, we were on our way downtown. Joe and I left our house with Moose, Dana's dog, and dropped him off with the parents of one of Dana's closest friends. How in the hell did we arrive safely at Sarah's place in downtown Chicago? Mercifully and miraculously, we drove down there without incident.

How were Joe and I dealing with this brutal, unbelievable nightmare? I saw how much Joe was suffering and I wanted us to hold each other and grieve together. But Joe could not let me in to share his pain. I felt like he could not handle receiving a hug from me nor giving me one. Because I was near emotional collapse myself, the message I took away was that, right or wrong, I was on my own to flounder through my unbearable sorrow and heartbreak without my husband. We each retreated into our own private hell on earth, tormented and shocked by Dana's murder.

We still had almost no details as we arrived downtown. When Sarah opened her door, my heart broke all over again. We clung to each other as if our lives depended on it, and I never wanted to let her go. As her mom, I yearned to take away her pain, but all I could do was be there with her as we began this unwanted journey together. After Sarah's friend left, we three huddled together not knowing what to do. Our little family was shattered, broken, never to be the same again. And when the three of us were finally together at Sarah's condo, she and I were still unsuccessful at getting Joe to let us comfort him and share his pain and sorrow.

Sarah questioned us about the murderer's name, saying that Dana's friend from college had been *Pat* Ford. Were we sure it was not him who had murdered her, the same "Pat" Dana told me she was meeting for the Cubs party the night before? Maybe the police had gotten the name wrong and it was not Joe Ford, but Pat Ford. I did not even want to think that might be true, because it seemed so much more horrific that a friend would have killed her.

We did not have to wait too much longer before talking to Detective Ed again. He had more information to share and questions to ask. The murderer *was* Patrick Ford. Dana had been found early Sunday morning in his apartment near Wrigleyville, the area around Wrigley Field in Chicago. She had been strangled and stabbed multiple times. Her murderer had called 911 and admitted he had killed someone. When the police had arrived, he had been waiting for them and said he had tried to kill himself. Patrick Ford had been taken to the hospital, and the detectives were waiting to question him again. Detective Ed asked what we knew about the murderer, but all I could share was what Dana had told me the day before and the vague memory that she had known him in college about five to six years earlier.

Yeah, right, he tried to kill himself. He's probably just planning his insanity defense! What kind of psycho monster does something like this?

Upon hearing all the gruesome details of her murder, the overwhelming anguish gripped my heart again and threatened to put me over the edge into an emotional meltdown. I was haunted and filled with such an intense, crushing pain to think of Dana suffering, terrified and defenseless, without me there to comfort her, to hold her, and to tell her how much I loved her. It killed me knowing she had died alone. To know my child had been strangled and then stabbed so many times inflicted a devastating emotional trauma that will last a lifetime. It cannot be erased from my mind. How was I going to survive this? Would I ever stop being tormented and haunted by how Dana had died and that I had not been there for her?

Reawakening

Right about that time, Rita called me back. She already knew Dana had been murdered and asked if we would like her to come over. Please, yes!

Thank you, God, for Rita. She'll know what to do; she'll help the three of us. She's known me for many years now and is familiar with our family dynamics. I know at least Sarah and I will be comforted by Rita's presence, even if for a little while.

Rita's calming presence soothed and comforted me that afternoon. That was all she could do. We grieved together for a while, taking solace in sharing our sorrow. What a gift that Rita wanted to be with our family as much as Sarah and I wanted to have her there with us. Joe greeted Rita and then spent most of his time in Sarah's bedroom while Rita was with us. Once she left, we had to face the grim reality that it was time to drive back out to the suburbs.

I don't really want to go home. But we should go back soon because there are people waiting for us, family and friends. I don't want to have to face anyone with the reality of what's happened. This just CAN'T be real! How can I survive this crushing, searing pain of knowing that my Dana was brutally murdered? God, please help me and help us!

With my help, Sarah packed her suitcase and, despondent, the three of us made the heartbreaking trek back home. We had been warned that news reporters were staking out our property, questioning neighbors and friends as they entered and left our house. Our plan was to call when we got close to our house and have someone open our garage door. Then we could enter our garage and close the door so as not to be harassed. Detective Ed had advised us to notify him if any reporter continued bothering us after we made our wishes known that none of us had even the slightest desire to speak with the news agencies. It never came to that, and we never spoke with a single reporter for the next several years.

CHAPTER 5

SEEING THE FACE OF GOD

How would Sarah, Joe, and I make it through this day, having to face and interact with those who had come to support us, to comfort us, to grieve with us? How would I bear seeing the immeasurable sadness and grief on their faces, a mirror image of what they saw on mine? My heart was broken and seemed beyond repair as we pulled into our garage. I did not know if I could stand any more pain that day.

Upon entering my kitchen late that Sunday afternoon, I **was** overwhelmed as we were greeted by family members and friends who had gathered throughout the day to be there for us. Overcome with emotion, I sensed this was exactly where I needed to be. Three of my siblings from Wisconsin—Tina, Mike, and Cindy—had driven down and were waiting to console us, hug us, and cry with us. Joe's two sisters, Linda and Angel, had phoned so many of our family and friends during the day even though they were in complete shock themselves. We had given them little information before leaving for Chicago that morning. As a result, they were confused about what had happened and where Dana had been murdered. Questions went unanswered for a while as this group cradled Sarah, Joe, and me in love and kindness. I so desperately needed that. They all took care of us. We did not have to think; we just existed and accepted their support.

We had returned home to a house filled with abundant love as well as almost unbearable sadness and grief. Yet just as it takes a village to raise a child, the power of the love of this small community of family and friends lifted me up and kept me from drowning in my sorrow that afternoon and early evening. I cannot speak for

Joe and Sarah here, but I have no doubt now I was seeing the face of God in everyone who grieved with us that day. In our darkest hours, our God is holding each one of us and walking with us. This group of relatives and friends had come to console us that horrible day and, in making that choice, had opened themselves by sharing our unbelievable pain and heartbreak. Each of them had given us a gift of themselves: their time and their heart. These were the first of our legion of angels, whose numbers exploded in the days and weeks to come. My faith tells me we were experiencing the comforting and healing presence of God through the physical presence of these special people in our lives, even from the beginning of this nightmare. I had prayed for God to help the three of us get through this day, and my prayers had been answered.

The stark differences in how Sarah, Joe, and I each grieved began to reveal themselves that day. Although I would come to accept there is no right or wrong way to grieve and that every individual needs to grieve in his or her own unique way, I was in no place emotionally to accept my husband shutting me out of whatever he was feeling. Why would Joe walk this terrifying journey alone, without Sarah and me? What I was not processing at all was that Joe was coping as best he could. If I had been more rational and able to comprehend that fact, I may have had more compassion toward Joe and I might have been spared some emotional trauma of my own. But I was far from rational, and as a result, those childhood feelings of abandonment and vulnerability had resurfaced.

In my gut, however, I knew I already had a network of "sisters." This extraordinary and loving group of women—my sisters, sisters-in-law, close girlfriends, and Sarah—had been there with me through two breast cancer diagnoses and many of life's twists and turns. I had no doubt those who could handle this unbearable emotional trauma would be there with me and for me, to grieve with me, to cry with me, and to share stories about Dana. But I also wanted my husband to walk with me through whatever was to come! And, from what I had already experienced that day, the odds of that happening did not seem promising.

Sarah grieved differently than Joe and me. As much as she needed some comfort and support from our relatives and friends, eventually she had had enough and wanted to be alone with her thoughts. Unlike Joe, she would not shut down emotionally, but she also had her limits as to how much she wanted to share and with whom.

As the evening wore on, even I was ready for some downtime from talking and from being "on" for hours. At the same time, I dreaded the moment when the last person would walk out our door and the three of us, lost souls, would be left alone in the silence of our individual grief and pain. I did not think there would be much sleeping in our house that night.

CHAPTER 6

THE FIRST NIGHT

Once that front door closed, the reality of our situation was impossible to ignore. There were no more visitors, no more phone calls to distract us. As the darkness of the summer evening descended, there was an unsettling quiet in the house and the darkness of the night mirrored the darkness of my soul.

How can my precious Dana be dead? Maybe she will just walk through our door. I just talked to her yesterday afternoon. I can't believe and do not want to accept what happened to her. It is impossible for my brain to imagine this possibility. But here we are, three zombies in a trance, not knowing what to do or how to act.

Finally left alone, no longer four but just the three of us, I could not be distracted anymore from all that had happened. The horror of our new reality was unfathomable to comprehend and absorb. Yet even in my anguish and despair, the truth could not be denied. We cried quietly, robotic and in shock, inconsolable and exhausted by our stress. There was nothing else to do but try to sleep. I hoped to find peace from the thoughts and pictures in my head of my murdered daughter. The three of us went to bed, Sarah in between Joe and me in our queen-sized bed, each of us lost in our own nightmarish hell on earth. This pattern continued for a few weeks because we could not bear to be apart when the darkness came each evening.

I do not remember if Sarah and Joe fell asleep quickly that night. I could not sleep as my mind replayed the last week or so over and over—our celebration party with the family about a week ago for Sarah and Dana and the fun we had had, the days and evenings spent with Dana when she'd gotten home from Minnesota, the conversations Dana and I had had on Saturday about the coffee table and about her going downtown to a party, the anguish and anger at myself for not being able to protect her (as if that were actually possible!), the night before when I had been awake all night worried about where she was and trying to remain calm, the phone call early Sunday morning that had ended our world as we knew it forever, the pictures I had in my head of my Dana, found lifeless after being murdered. There was no consoling me as I wept softly, trying hard to keep from sobbing so as not to wake Joe or Sarah.

And then in my despair, I felt it! I felt a soft, almost feathery touch on my left shoulder. It lingered for only a second or two, such a brief yet calming touch. Then it was gone so quickly that I almost did not think it had really happened.

What was THAT?! It could not have been Sarah or Joe. They're asleep and neither of them is on my left! Oh my God! That was my Dana, telling me that she is okay!

That fleeting, gentle touch on my shoulder, that miraculous moment, soothed me a bit and helped me to meditate on that which I already believed from my faith—that our lives do not end forever when we leave this earth, that for eternity we can be with a Father who loves us unconditionally, that we can have everlasting life where we will be reunited with our loved ones. I had found some small comfort earlier that day, believing my Dana was in heaven with her God and Father, at peace and watching over us. But my experiencing that light, feathery touch was truly a moment of grace. In that most miraculous instant, I received an unbelievable gift—a gift that reinforced my belief that Dana *was* at peace and with her God, a gift that consoled me as I trusted she was there with me in my pain and sorrow, a gift that reminded me someday, hopefully, I will be with my daughter again in heaven.

CHAPTER 7

TAKING CARE OF BUSINESS

Little did I realize all that had to be organized in the next several days to plan a funeral and burial for Dana. When my dad had died six weeks earlier, I had not been able to travel to Green Bay to help with the planning because I had been recovering from surgery. I would have been sad and the planning would have been difficult because we had all been dealing with our father's death. Yet I cannot imagine there is anything worse than having to plan your child's burial. My dad had led a long life and had been failing for years. Our daughter had been murdered at a most promising time in her young life and her life had been snuffed out in an instant. The business of planning a funeral was exhausting and kept us busy from Monday morning through Friday that week.

How were we able to do everything? Reflecting on that week, it is difficult to believe we survived the stress, exhaustion, and all-encompassing grief. Just when I thought I might not have the emotional toughness to survive this tragedy, somewhere from deep within I found the strength and determination to complete each task, one at a time, until everything was finished. Being in shock and feeling numb helped me get through these days. But it was my strong desire to have Dana's spirit and presence there with us at the visitation and the funeral mass that kept me going during the entire week.

Every day presented a new challenge. Among the many tasks that needed to be done were choosing a funeral home, picking out a casket, writing an obituary, planning a visitation, and choosing a date for the funeral mass. Then we had to decide on a cemetery for burial, pick out a specific burial plot, meet with a bereavement counselor at our church to plan the funeral mass, choose an outfit for Dana to be buried in, and identify our daughter's body at Cook County Morgue. This is what awaited us as we began our lives without Dana.

Monday morning dawned. Unprepared and filled with apprehension, Joe, Sarah, and I drove to a local funeral home to begin the business of burying our daughter and sister. Joe chose the funeral home because he had planned his dad's services there years earlier. Here we met Jim, a most kind, calm, and caring funeral director, who explained his part in this whole process and how he would guide us through it all, step by step. Jim gently walked us through every detail that morning. The first decisions we had to make were whether Dana would be cremated and whether she would be buried in the ground or a mausoleum.

My God, whoever thinks of these things in advance for their child? What should we do? I have no idea! This is the last place any of us wants to be.

Sarah informed us of a conversation she'd had with Dana as they had driven home from Green Bay after my dad's funeral. Dana had been emphatic about never wanting to be buried in the ground! Great, we had our answer. Dana would be buried in a mausoleum somewhere.

With Jim's guidance that morning, we composed the obituary, agreed on the dates for the visitation and the funeral, and chose the casket. Joe was firm about wanting the visitation and funeral to take place in the next few days. However, we needed several days to allow for my family to arrive from all over the country. They would be traveling from California, Colorado, and Georgia, as well as from Wisconsin. There was also the issue of an autopsy to be performed on Dana and the question of exactly when the funeral home would begin preparing her body for the visitation. As much as delaying the visitation and funeral, even for one day, went against Joe's wishes, I wanted and needed my family to be there with me. An extra few days would allow for their travel time. Finally, we compromised on a one-day visitation on Thursday and the funeral mass at St. James Catholic Church, our parish church, on Friday. At Jim's suggestion, we chose a restaurant for a luncheon after the funeral.

When it was time to choose the casket, Joe stayed in the office as Jim, Sarah, and I walked downstairs to view our choices. Entering that room, where all the caskets were on display, was one of the most difficult moments for me at the funeral home that morning.

I can't believe we are picking out a casket for Dana! Why can I not wake up from this horrible nightmare? Why, why do we have to do this?

Sarah and I wandered around the room aimlessly at first, dazed and devastated by the task before us. We must have drawn strength from each other, though, because soon we agreed on a simple, beautiful, dusty rose–colored casket that seemed perfect for our Dana. Weirdly, as I am writing this, I remember now a feeling of comfort and peace washing over me then, as Sarah and I lovingly chose the vessel in which Dana's body would be buried. At the time, I was not able to realize that small gift that soothed my soul for just a moment. As I write this, tears fill my eyes and I am overwhelmed with the emotions that have surfaced with this memory. Even then, in my deepest despair, I was being held and consoled in the loving arms of a God and Father who always takes care of us. Before leaving the funeral home that morning, we discussed cemetery options. That decision was an easy one. We chose All Saints Catholic Cemetery, which was near our house and familiar to us. That seemed important at the time. Jim called to inform their staff we would be visiting that afternoon and prepared them with our story. Joe chose not to accompany Sarah and me, so the two of us headed over to the cemetery. Sadly, I acquiesced. I did not have the energy or desire to fight for what I wanted. What I wanted was for my husband to help us in all this! I was in no place to even consider the possibility that Joe was unable to share any part of himself with anyone. In hindsight, I understand and accept that my husband was trying to keep from drowning, just like me but in his own way, from the unrelenting grief.

With every task we checked off our list that morning, another small piece of my heart shattered. Thank God Sarah and I could support each other. She and I are so much alike in that we do not shy away from difficult or painful situations. We may fight it for a time, but in the end, we will do what needs to be done and deal with the emotional fallout as necessary. Now, even in our overwhelming sadness and grief, together Sarah and I found the strength and courage to move through this day and take care of our Dana in the only way we could. Nevertheless, I was becoming more annoyed with Joe as this day went on.

Father Jim, the young priest who would celebrate Dana's funeral mass, stopped by Monday evening with two prayer shawls for Sarah and me. The prayer shawl ministry at St. James creates a wide variety of shawls for anyone in need of prayers or blessings. What touching gifts these were for Sarah and me when we most needed to be comforted. Father Jim shared a meal with us that evening. I so enjoyed getting to know him better and sharing with him stories of our lives with Dana. He was interested in getting to know her in a more personal way.

Tuesday's tasks were no less daunting than the day before and were just as necessary. Sometime Monday afternoon, the funeral director had called to inform us the autopsy on Dana was complete. Someone needed to go down to the Cook County Morgue in Chicago on Tuesday to identify Dana's body for them to release her to the funeral home. As we discussed who would go, Joe's response was almost immediate. He would not go and suggested sending a friend. He did not want any of us to have to go through the agony of that experience. As much as I understood his reasoning, I could not imagine sending a friend to identify Dana. Without hesitation, I made my decision. This was my daughter, and as horrendous as it might be, I wanted to be the one to identify her. Joe tried to talk me out of it, but I was adamant and undeterred. My two sisters-in-law, Linda and Angel, would accompany me.

I want Joe to come with me to identify Dana's body. This is OUR daughter and I need him to be there with me! I understand he doesn't want to accept this nightmarish reality. But what about me? How could he NOT understand this would be horrible for me too? Why should I have to do this without my husband?

My disappointment and anger continued to increase because I wanted Joe's support in the most difficult thing we may ever need to do as parents. I listened and observed as Sarah struggled with her decision to join us or not. In the end, she was torn but decided she did not want to have that image of her sister in her head forever. Why could I be so understanding and accepting of Sarah's decision but be angry about Joe's? This says much more about me, in my emotionally vulnerable state, than about Joe. In my own suffering and unbearable heartbreak, I could not accept at the time that my life partner could not share his grief with me and did not want to walk with me in dealing with all that had to be done.

On the other hand, Sarah was my daughter and I wanted to protect her from any more heartache. She and I were in a healthy place in our relationship. We are kindred spirits in that regard; we can generally share our true feelings with each other and we have a wonderful, strong mother-daughter bond. I sensed she struggled with her decision partly because she wanted to go to support me and partly because she wondered if she would regret seeing Dana at the morgue. I accepted her decision without anger or sadness. This dichotomy, my contradicting reactions, speaks clearly to me of the ability of my daughter to be present emotionally even in the most painful of situations. This contrasted with what I perceived at the time as Joe's inability to be open to share our pain and sorrow with each other.

I called the funeral home to tell Jim who would make the trip to the morgue to identify Dana. Compassionate as he is, Jim offered to drive us there on Tuesday morning. We had no idea what to expect. I steeled myself as best as I could for the task ahead. I could only imagine it being like what I had seen on TV or in the movies. I had this picture of Dana's beautiful face being all beaten and bruised, or slashed. I am not sure if I knew then that she had died of strangulation, but I knew she had also been stabbed multiple times. I did not know then where the stabbings were. Horrible images kept flashing through my head, just imagining the scenario.

Why do I feel the need to do this? Because I am her mom and I would do anything to take care of her in whatever way is necessary. And I have a desperate need to see my baby girl. Can I deal with the pain and nightmares if it is more than I can handle? Maybe by seeing her, I can put to rest this anguish I can't let go of because I could not be with her at the crime scene.

During the brief yet seemingly endless wait, the gruesome slideshow of images in my mind never stopped. As the three of us were ushered into a small room, I was still numb with shock, feeling as if I were in a trance. Dana was not there. Where was she? The representative explained we would view Dana on the video monitor on the wall and identify her that way. For a fleeting moment, before the screen came on, sadness washed over me. I would not be able to touch my child even for a few seconds. Suddenly, there she was on the video monitor, all covered except for her face. I felt like I had been punched in the gut. Could my broken heart withstand any more of this relentless, searing pain?

How can this be happening to me? How does anyone survive this process of identifying their loved one at a morgue? God help me!

There she was, my baby girl, with her eyes closed and her hair all pulled back and bunched up and matted behind her head. The three of us held each other, crying. I did not want to leave her, even though it was just an image on a video monitor! This finalized for me that she was dead—not that I had any doubts. It is so hard to believe, but I felt a sense of relief because the pictures I'd had in my head were so much worse than the reality of what I witnessed on that video monitor.

As we left that depressing place, the four of us silently walked back to Jim's car. On the drive home the mood was somber and quiet. The exhaustion of the last several days allowed me to close my eyes and nap for most of the ride. When we arrived at the funeral home, Jim commented that he would bring Dana back home later that day and that she would be beautiful the next time we saw her.

For a moment, in my state of shock, I was ecstatic but confused, thinking she was coming home alive! Of course, the brutal reality sunk in as I absorbed what he meant. How could he *ever* think I would see Dana as beautiful, in death? But I was filled with gratitude. Trusting that she would be lovingly brought back home to Arlington Heights comforted me. I did not want to think about her remaining in the cold, harsh, sterile, and anonymous environment of a morgue.

Later that same Tuesday afternoon, Joe and I headed over to our church to meet with our bereavement counselor to design Dana's funeral mass. There was no rest for the weary in this business. Our counselor's job was to help us choose the songs as well as the first and second readings from the Bible. She guided us through the order of the funeral mass (also called the Mass of the Resurrection) and when necessary, gave us samples of readings and songs to choose from. We needed to give her the names of the pallbearers, the readers, those who would bring up the offertory gifts, and someone to possibly share words of remembrance in celebrating Dana's life. Because it meant so much to me, I gave much consideration as to whom I would ask to participate in each of those jobs.

Finally, Joe must have been unable to bear this task any longer as he got up and walked out of that room, saying he would wait for me outside. I am sure our bereavement counselor understood Joe's coping mechanism in a way I was not able to comprehend or accept at the time. Trying to block that all out, however, I focused instead on the job of designing Dana's funeral mass, choosing the participants as well as the songs and readings that deeply touched me.

I am so sad at the way I reacted to Joe's grief back then. In the depth of my own grief, though, I simply could not understand how he seemed to be so completely closed off. Thinking back on those first days, I can only conclude that Joe was protecting himself from his own crushing, unbearable sorrow as best he could; nothing and no one was going to penetrate that wall he had erected! I sensed Joe was in as much pain as I was, but I could not accept that he would shut me out as each of us was suffering. I had a lot to learn.

When I was trying to decide on the person best fit to share words of Dana's life journey, there was only one candidate I even considered, and that was my psychotherapist, Rita. Not only had she been my therapist, but Dana had also been her patient from the time she was nine years old until she was about twenty for her panic attacks and panic disorder. I saw my child blossom, from being almost paralyzed at times with panic attacks throughout those many years, into a confident young woman who pursued her goals in life and was on her way to veterinary school. Rita could speak of Dana's courage through her adversities as well as of how she had grown into the knowledge of herself in relationship with others. And who better to give us a glimpse of the young woman Dana had been on the inside?

Throughout these several days of preparation, at home we were surrounded by family, friends, and neighbors stopping by to comfort us, bring us meals, offer their help when needed, and just be present with us in our grief and sorrow. They supplied us with meals, snacks, water, pop, coffee, tea, plastic cups, silverware, tissues, and every other type of paper product imaginable, and they kept things organized in our household. But the most thoughtful and treasured gifts they each brought were their presence along with their love and compassion. Our family was richly blessed with the outpouring of love and support from these people.

All who graced us with their presence were among that legion of angels whose numbers continued to multiply. Father Jim, in his homily at the funeral mass later that week, said, "If numbers alone could heal, then the massive outpouring of love and solidarity and support for Dana's family during the past few days and again today would have expelled their every sorrow and dried their last tear. I went over to see Joe, Barb, and Sarah this past Monday night. I do not know what I was expecting to find, *but* my expectations were blown away at the amount of food and number of people present in the Mangi home both mourning and remembering Dana in tears, laughter, and stories." I will be ever thankful for the constant love and support that was showered on Joe, Sarah, and me in our time of intense sorrow and loss.

Reawakening

Wednesday's formidable task was to choose our favorite photos of Dana throughout her life—those by herself, with Sarah, with Joe and me, as a family, with her many different groups of friends, with her cousins, aunts and uncles, with her dogs (Moose and Riley). In the meantime, a few of Dana's closest girlfriends were in the process of doing the same with photos of their favorite times together. They would add their photo boards to ours at the visitation the next day. By now I was drained from all that had been accomplished in the past several days. Even so, I made the photo boards and gathered the songs and pictures to include in a video presentation, because that was important to me. Thank God for my many helpers as Sarah, my sister Cindy, and several of Dana's closest girlfriends worked with me to make these photo boards a celebration of Dana's life. This was our gift of love to our daughter, sister, niece, and girlfriend.

Several of Dana's closest girlfriends had asked us to let them do something special to help. Jim had called earlier in the week requesting an outfit for Dana to be buried in. His only requirement was the outfit should have long sleeves and a high neck. What a perfect task to give Dana's girlfriends. With their love and sense of Dana's style, I had no doubt they would choose a most beautiful outfit for her. That would be their gift to us and to their "sister" at heart.

The casket would be open to family for an hour before the general visitation began. I needed to see my Dana, and I sensed there were some in our two families who would feel the same way, if given the option. Joe, Sarah, and I compromised, deciding on the private viewing to give our families and a few friends the opportunity to say goodbye to Dana and spend that time with her before the general visitation began. Then the casket would be closed during the general visitation per Joe's wishes.

Amidst these days of planning and grieving, of trying to stay busy to avoid the silence and yet needing the quiet to settle and rest our weary minds and bodies, we got some more shocking news. The medical examiner had discovered severe heart disease in Dana while performing her autopsy. It was so advanced that she had about a 90 percent blockage in her left main coronary artery. Because that is quite rare in a twenty-five-year-old in good health, the medical examiner quickly relayed the message that she felt it was imperative for the three of us to get tested for heart disease as soon as possible! She, along with one of our family physicians, was most concerned about Sarah, wondering whether she might have the same condition as Dana. As astonishing and scary as this news was, any testing on us would have to wait until after Dana's funeral mass on Friday. Sarah and I made appointments to get our heart scans the day after Dana's funeral mass. It took every fiber of my being to not succumb to the terror gripping me as I imagined losing my Sarah from heart disease. But, first things first—the visitation and funeral for Dana loomed ahead and threatened to finally crush my spirit.

Oh my God, how much more can we endure? I think I will crumble and die if I lose another daughter. I do not want to die either!

I can't deal with all of this now, not until I get through the next two days. But it is imperative we get an appointment as soon as possible. Thank God Joe had a CT heart scan recently and his results showed no plaque in his arteries.

CHAPTER 8

HEART WRENCHING YET COMFORTING

Thursday morning arrived with a sense of dread and anticipation. That entire week, including the night Dana died, the Chicago area had been dealing with severe summer weather of heavy rains and power outages. To me, it seemed like the heavens were crying for us and with us as well as lashing out at Dana's murderer. This day was no exception. It was hot, humid, and there was a threat of severe storms later in the day. With breaking hearts, Sarah and I left for the funeral home. Joe would follow us later, after the casket had been closed.

Having that private hour with an open casket gave Sarah and me the time we so desperately needed. I am not sure either one of us could have survived the walk up to the casket alone, but together we faced our most dreaded nightmare. I experienced so many intense feelings in those first few moments of seeing my lifeless, beloved daughter. I rode an emotional roller coaster, from the depths of unrelenting despair, sorrow, and hopelessness that threatened to swallow me, to the feeling of my broken heart spilling over with a mother's love and tenderness for my child. Sarah and I supported each other, crying softly, as we gently touched Dana's silky hair, her beautiful face and her hands, as we kissed her and simply spent that time being near her before the casket was closed and the room was opened to the public. With abundant gratitude, I recognized Jim had truly given me a gift. I would never, ever have thought I could feel this way, but Dana *did* look beautiful to me that afternoon. This image of my Dana, at peace, was his gift to replace the image

I had in my head of how she had looked when I identified her at Cook County Morgue. Several of my siblings, my nieces and nephews, Joe's sisters, and the few friends we invited to come early could grieve with us as we comforted each other and drew strength from each other. I hoped for all of us who loved Dana that this private visitation time would be healing and would help us to get some closure.

Once the doors were opened for general visitation, hundreds of visitors lined up throughout the six hours, all there to comfort us and grieve with us. The mix of people that day was amazing; they included our extended families, personal family friends, work colleagues from current and past jobs, Sarah's friends all the way from grade school through graduate school as well as her work friends, Dana's friends from grade school through graduate school and even a few new friends from the University of Minnesota Veterinary College, acquaintances, and even strangers. The outpouring of support was truly overwhelming, especially because severe weather came through the Chicago metropolitan area in the late afternoon. Tornado sirens blared as all of us were ushered downstairs at the funeral home for ten to fifteen minutes. When all was clear, we continued with the visitation. However, power was out all over the metro area. Huge trees were down, many of them blocking roadways and driveways. Basements were flooding, yet even with these obstacles, people poured into the funeral home. Many had driven for hours in the Chicago area just to get out to our suburb and several people had driven through the terrible weather from other states to be there with us. Even some of the Chicago police who had heard about the murder or had been assigned to the case came to pay their respects and shared with us how Dana's murder had deeply affected them.

Thursday was an excruciatingly long day. After many hours of greeting people, I did not feel like I could even cry anymore. I was drained emotionally and physically, yet the loving support of the community of friends and family strengthened me and held me up throughout that day and evening. As exhausted as I was, my spirit was lifted a bit each time I was greeted and/or embraced by a guest who had come to grieve with us and maybe share a short story about Dana with me. Mercifully, by about 10:00 p.m., we could finally go home and attempt to get some sleep. I was not looking forward to the funeral and burial service the next morning, as the finality of those upcoming events was not lost on me.

How am I going to survive that final closing of the casket, that final goodbye to my Dana? I don't want to say goodbye!

As Friday dawned, the destruction from the severe storms the night before was all around us. Many streetlights around Arlington Heights and its surrounding suburbs were still out. Streets everywhere were flooded, making traffic almost impossible in some areas. Getting around was proving to be difficult this morning. Luckily, we lived close to the funeral home.

Anyone who wanted to proceed to the church with us met at the funeral home for a final prayer. Those who were invited to see Dana one more time had a few minutes of privacy before the casket was closed and the doors were open to the public. Once everyone was settled, instructions were given about the processional to the church. Then, from the back row to the front, each person filed past the casket to say their farewell. Witnessing each person's unique farewell was not only heart wrenching, but touching. What a tribute to the spirit of this beautiful, loving young woman whom I am honored to call my daughter. To this day, I can clearly picture the tender farewell of my brother, Dan. He brought his hands together in front of his heart, as if in prayer, and made a respectful, slow bow to Dana. It was several years later, when I started yoga, that I learned at the end of a class our teacher would bring us into a seated position, have us bring our hands together at our hearts, and as he or she bowed to us, would say, "Namaste." We, the students, would respond in kind. The word *namaste* literally means "I bow to you," but my favorite definition is "The light in me honors the light in you." Dan's gesture has always affected me deeply, even more when I think of my brother saying "Namaste" to his niece in farewell to her.

Finally, the three of us, her immediate family, painfully walked up to Dana's casket. As I followed Joe out of the room, I realized Sarah was still at her sister's side, sobbing and refusing to leave Dana. We had to gently escort her away to the car to start the procession to the church. I could not bear seeing my Sarah in such excruciating agony and distress, yet there was nothing I could do to lighten her burden. All I could do was put my arms around her and hold her close, letting her know she was not alone.

The short ride to the church was quiet and somber. As we approached the parking lot, I was amazed at the number of cars that were already there, in addition to the many that were part of our procession. Our limousine came around to the front of the church to drop us off. Just before we got out of the car, the funeral director approached the limo to inform us our luncheon had been cancelled. The restaurant had no power from the previous night's storms. Jim said he would try to find another venue for us. When Joe responded that we did not need a luncheon, Sarah and I thought differently and asked Jim to pursue looking for another option. My sense was that Joe had found this news a relief; he was going to avoid a luncheon after all! But for me personally, I desperately wanted to spend time with and thank the wonderful community of family and friends who had supported us throughout this nightmare by inviting them to share a meal with our family. As much as I had felt the panic rising in me when I had first heard Jim's announcement, he was so calm and compassionate in caring for our every need that I trusted him to do his best. Then I refocused on what was to come as we exited the car and prepared to proceed into church behind the casket and the pallbearers.

As we walked into the church and began the processional, it took all the strength I had left to keep from collapsing under the weight of the sorrow and grief that was breaking my heart and crushing my spirit. Our beautiful little church was overflowing with mourners, there for Dana and there to grieve with us and pray with us. I was in awe of this remarkable support system, this community of family and friends who were all there to share with us this intimate, heartrending, yet moving celebration of Dana's life and her new life with God. The massive amount of love and friendship I felt in the church that horribly sad day was what I would hold on to as I began my new life without my Dana. This was our network of family and friends who would continue to surround us with love and compassion in the days, weeks, and months to come.

The processional stopped toward the back of the church for the rite called the Placing of the Pall. It is said to be a most tender moment in the Catholic funeral Mass. When the casket enters the church, the priest sprinkles it with holy water. Then a large white cloth, the pall, may be placed upon it in silence. The pall recalls the white baptismal garment that Catholics each receive at baptism as a sign of their Christian dignity. The pall also signifies equality and challenges people who form judgments based on how someone is dressed. The funeral pall clothes every deceased Christian in the same garment. Indeed, for me it was a most tender moment, as three of Dana's cousins were able to participate in this final gesture, symbolically clothing Dana in the garments she would wear before the throne of God.

We then continued up the middle aisle behind Dana's casket. I saw the blur of faces but could not make eye contact, knowing I would surely break down if I did. I was focusing all my energy on holding Sarah up as we walked slowly to the front pew. Joe and I slid into our seats, and I expected Sarah to be right behind me. But when I turned to her, she was still out in the aisle standing just behind the casket, sobbing. Someone had to gently pry her away and helped her into the pew next to me. How many ways could my heart be broken and continue beating?

The funeral Mass included meaningful Bible readings and songs, the homily given by Father Jim, and the general intercession prayers for Dana, for all family members and friends, for the sick, the elderly and the poor, for all family members who had died, for peace in our families, and for peace in the world. The liturgy of the Mass then continued as usual until the end of the service when Rita came forward to share her remembrance of Dana. As the Mass ended, we filed out of church behind Dana's casket and waited in the car as the procession for the short journey to the cemetery was organized.

Our slow, reverent, 150-car funeral procession traveled with a police escort from St. James Church to the cemetery that Friday morning. Part of our route traveled through storm-ravaged areas, where police officers were already busy managing many intersections with failed stoplights. As we approached, these officers gave a respectful, clear pass to Dana's procession. During the short service at the cemetery, I reached for Joe's hand at one point and he quickly pulled it away.

Oh my God! He can't bear to be touched by me. I feel like I am poisonous. Not only have I cruelly lost my daughter, but Joe is lost to me too. I am drowning here and I do not know how to save myself . . . It is too painful to think about right now.

Jim had miraculously put together a funeral luncheon for us at another venue while we were in church that morning. The restaurant was scheduled to hold a wedding reception later that afternoon but scrambled to put together a nice lunch for our party. Their only requirement was that we needed to get everyone out of the room at a certain time for their staff to have time to set up for the wedding reception. Sharing a meal in community with these family members and friends, to thank them all for being there for us during the previous week and to spend some time with them in a more relaxing setting, comforted me greatly. Once the luncheon was over, we said our goodbyes to everyone. That concluded the official funeral obligations for our family.

Sarah and Joe headed home to rest while I took my siblings and their families back to the cemetery. From the moment Sarah and I had been shown the Immaculate Heart of Mary Garden Mausoleum at All Saints Catholic Cemetery earlier that week, I had experienced a sense of peacefulness and serenity in the beauty of the setting. I knew instantly this was where I wanted my Dana to rest. With the splashing of the fountain, the soothing trickling of the tiny waterfall in the pond, and the explosion of nature's magnificent colors from the myriad flora surrounding the mausoleum, I felt I was standing on holy ground. This sacred, beautiful space continues to help soothe and calm me whenever I visit Dana. My family all wanted to see where Dana's body was to rest, and I was grateful to share this tranquil resting place with them. Together we all comforted each other as best we could in our brokenness and in our overwhelming grief.

All my siblings and their families would be staying close by for another night before returning to their homes. From the cemetery, I returned home to rest for a few hours. Once home, I realized I did not want to stay away from my family of origin that evening. If I had never thought about it before this week, I now understood so clearly what a gift it is to have siblings to share in my joyful and unbelievably painful moments. Even though I was emotionally and physically exhausted, I longed to spend some time with them, knowing we'd all be saying goodbye the next day. I wanted to draw energy and strength from them—from their unconditional love, from the hugs I yearned for and knew I would receive, from the knowledge that they were there for me no matter what and would not pull away from me. Sarah joined me, and for that short while, we could bask in the companionship we all shared, and just be. There were no expectations, and nothing more was required of us. After many hugs and some tears, we said good night, and I made plans to meet them for breakfast.

I hadn't been able to imagine how I was going to survive that first week with everything that needed to be planned as well as attending the visitation and the funeral Mass. With God's help and the extraordinary, loving embrace of an amazing community of family, friends, acquaintances, and strangers, I had survived it all. Although the funeral Mass had been an extremely sad reminder of the finality of Dana's life here with us, it was also such a moving, uplifting, and personal tribute to her life and her beautiful spirit. I needed that experience more than I could ever have imagined.

Father Jim's homily had touched so many people of all faiths that day and some with little or no faith at all. He honestly expressed his struggles after he had received the horrible news from Joe on Sunday morning:

"I have struggled with death, with evil, with pain, suffering, with comforting, hope, goodness, faith and resurrection. I along with most of you have perhaps struggled with these thoughts this week. Why did God allow this to happen? Why? Maybe, though, as I woke this morning, we have been struggling and trying to answer the wrong question or questions. All our energy has been focused on why. I'd like to think we should be focusing on the question: *Now what?* If you had the chance to view the video at the wake, you heard the Josh Groban song 'Don't Give Up.' Those words struck me. Driving home, praying, sleeping, and getting up—Don't give up! Don't give up! Dana wouldn't, and neither should we! We are all the better for ever having known her. I think this is Dana speaking to each one of us today—be strong, determined, unafraid of the future, ready to meet every challenge, believe in ourselves and try and keep believing in God, even if that seems to be difficult right now, right here. Dana was not rich, but she left a legacy. In fact, she left a treasury, a treasury of love. This past week I have seen and felt that treasury opened. Now what? Don't give up! Today is the first day of Dana's new life and the first day of the rest of our lives."

He was able to draw everyone together as a community, no matter what their religion or beliefs, to celebrate Dana's life and to pray for her and for all present that day. Many of our family and friends shared with me how moved they were by his homily, his humor, his compassion, and his ability to touch each one of them personally.

Rita's tribute to Dana was equally as touching. She too was able to draw us all together to reflect on, remember, and celebrate Dana's life. As I listened to Rita describe Dana's life journey—the courage she showed through all the adversity she faced, her growth in the knowledge of herself in relation to others, and the gradual acceptance of herself as an imperfect yet lovable person—I knew I had chosen the best person to speak about my cherished daughter. Rita spoke emotionally of all Dana had accomplished in her twenty-five years. She helped us remember the beautiful person Dana had been on the inside: courageous, resilient, funny, persistent, empathetic, spiritual, maddeningly stubborn at times, forgiving, and loving. I needed to hear those accolades to give me something to smile about, if even for just a moment. Many at that Mass later talked with me about how moved they were by Rita's eulogy and how she so eloquently captured the essence of Dana's beautiful, strong spirit.

A few months later, when I was able to reflect on how Dana's funeral Mass had affected me, I recognized in a most powerful way why a funeral Mass is so important in our faith. Being fully present in the moment, that sacred Mass had given me the opportunity to grieve and cry. It had comforted me, it had helped me remember and made me smile, and it had left me with a most beautiful vision of Dana being welcomed home by our heavenly Father. I never professed to understanding why this happened, but I believed then, and I still do, that Dana was at peace and she was in a safe place where she could not be hurt anymore.

These two wonderful speakers, Father Jim and Rita, were our gifts from God, given to walk with us in our grief, in our pain, in our sadness, in our shock, in our hope, and finally, in our celebration of Dana's short life here with us. Their heartfelt and sincere words touched me in such a profound way that they would continue to guide me as I moved through my healing journey in the difficult days and months ahead.

CHAPTER 9

THE AFTERMATH

I was shocked that I did not die from grief. And I know now that I will not die from it, because I choose not to. I may run, or shake wildly, or lie paralyzed on the ground for a while, but I will not ultimately succumb.

—Molly Fumia

Since all my family was leaving the day after the funeral, I looked forward to spending more time with some of them for breakfast that morning. It can be quite daunting, noisy, and overwhelming to be a part of my large extended family at any type of family function. Weddings and funerals seemed to be the only time we all got together anymore. This day, though, I welcomed the distraction. It was preferable to staying home in the uncomfortable atmosphere of pervading silence and tension, as the three of us each struggled with our self-imposed imprisonment of feelings, thoughts, memories, and questions. Eating breakfast together with my siblings' families also kept me from worrying about the heart scans Sarah and I would have later that morning. As I left the restaurant, I said my goodbyes to those who were headed home. The rest of us planned on meeting at my house to take a nice, leisurely walk on this warm, sunny day after Sarah and I returned from our tests.

Unbelievably, just one day after the emotional turmoil of Dana's funeral, Sarah and I had scans of the heart done. Her arteries looked good and seemed to have no blockages. Thank God! I was ecstatic that Sarah's results were fine. The thought of losing my other daughter was more than I could bear. On the other hand, I was told my score was 404 out of a range of 0–400! I was advised by what I experienced as a robotic, uncaring technician that if I was having trouble breathing or had chest pains, I should go immediately to the hospital. I began hyperventilating and just wanted to get the hell out of that room! Sarah could tell I was horribly upset. I could barely explain what had just happened, as I was shaking and in shock. I had been under the care of a cardiologist for years for elevated cholesterol, but I had never had any cardiac test results this serious. We decided Sarah should drive us home because I needed to call my cardiologist immediately and ask him what I should do. We were both so frightened. I could not bear the thought of leaving Sarah or of how my death would affect her after all she had just been through.

My wonderful cardiologist, Dr. L, called me back almost immediately on his day off and reassured me he was not too concerned for several reasons: I explained to him I was not having chest pains, I was not having trouble breathing, I had been training for a challenging bike trip to Italy in a month, and I had no symptoms when I exercised at a high level for several hours. In turn, he explained that although my test score appeared very alarming to me, it could indicate I had a little bit of plaque spread throughout my arteries as opposed to a lot of plaque in any one artery that would cause a problem. Lastly, we discussed the fact that I had just passed a cardiac stress test with flying colors in June 2007, about two months earlier, to get cleared for a minor surgery I needed. But just to be cautious, we scheduled an angiogram for the following Thursday to clearly see my arteries. I trusted Dr. L's judgment and was calmed by his assessment, especially because I *did* feel good and asymptomatic. But a little seed of worry had been planted in my head about what might be going on, so I was glad that I would go through this "gold standard" of tests to check the condition of my arteries the following week.

I had also called Joe with the news while I was still in the car. Scared for Sarah and me, he called his internist, who is also our friend, to get some reassurance and some information from him about both my surprising situation and Sarah's good outcome. By the time Sarah and I returned home, the news had spread and there was much apprehension among Joe and my family members, who had arrived to take a walk with me. The most shocking thing was that I might have severely clogged arteries even though I had exhibited no symptoms, but I felt less anxious after talking to Dr. L. The medical examiner had been so much more concerned about Sarah having the same severe heart disease that they had discovered in Dana during her autopsy. However, one thing was undeniable: from this moment on, our family history of heart disease that had been found in Dana must now be taken into consideration in both of our cases. The cardiologists were being proactive because of that.

I was reassured that Sarah's cardiologist scheduled a much more conclusive, detailed CT scan in the next week to get a clearer picture of her heart and arteries. Sarah's cholesterol levels had been elevated for a while already back in 2007 even though she was very fit, not at all overweight, and followed a healthy diet. This less invasive test was more appropriate for someone Sarah's age, who showed no cardiac symptoms. Early that next week the results of her CT scan were normal. Thank God!

I would be relieved after I had my angiogram, hoping to get a clean bill of health and get answers to all the questions nagging me. Until then I would try to put it out of my mind. This little scare, however, made it that much more difficult to say goodbye to the rest of my siblings that afternoon. They had been a huge part of my support system for the past couple of days. No matter what our differences (every family has them and mine is no different), my siblings and I have a strong bond and I wished they did not live so far away. I would certainly feel the loss of their presence and companionship as I struggled to find my way in this unwanted new life I now had to navigate.

The thought of being alone again—just Joe, Sarah, and me—was terrifying. For the past six days, I had kept myself constantly busy. Therefore, it had been relatively easy to avoid dealing with my wide range of heightened emotions. But now the overwhelming feelings of emptiness, hopelessness, and longing for Dana threatened to suck me into a bottomless pit from which I could not escape. Would I even want to escape? Truthfully, at times I was tempted to let my mind slide into blissful oblivion, into a state of absolute forgetfulness or unawareness, where I could avoid all this unrelenting, heartbreaking pain.

I saw the three of us as zombies, just existing, numb with grief, and each handling it in our own way. What would we do? How would we survive? Could we support each other in our unbearable loss? Because of my perception of Joe's absence, those pesky feelings of frustration, abandonment, and resentment that had been building in me all week persisted. I had no idea yet how to save myself from drowning in my sadness and loneliness.

For a brief instant, allowing my mind to quietly slip into peaceful oblivion seemed like a great solution. But this was not who I was! I had always been a fighter and had summoned the strength and courage to fight through many adversities. Now more than ever, I would need to summon that inner strength for this battle. Sarah and I had each other to lean on. I would *not* give up, because my Sarah needed me as much as I needed her. Sadly, I had no idea what Joe needed, or for that matter, what he wanted. So, I felt that avenue of support was not going to be available, and he didn't appear to want any comfort or support from me.

CHAPTER 10

REALLY, GOD?

    Almost one week after Dana's funeral, I was at the hospital to have the angiogram procedure. As the surgery nurses were preparing me, one of the questions they asked in obtaining my history was if I had been under any stress lately! Although it was painfully difficult to speak about, I felt it was prudent to inform them of my daughter's murder. That event alone probably put me over the top of their stress-meter measurement. Thankfully, I was given a drug similar to Valium to calm me before I even went into the cardiac-catheterization lab. A caring nurse introduced himself once I was in the room where the angiogram would be performed. He would be monitoring me during the procedure to make sure I remained comfortable and calm. I was told it was critical that I stay still and calm, as the cardiologist would be threading a catheter (a thin, flexible tube) up my artery through the groin to the heart. If I moved too much, the doctor could tear the artery.

    Dr. S, the cardiologist who would be performing my angiogram, came into the room and introduced himself. We discussed my medical history, my fitness level, my lack of symptoms, and what the procedure would involve. He was so compassionate and understanding as I told him about Dana. He explained he would look at my coronary arteries, and if he saw plaque buildup narrowing any artery and dangerously reducing its blood flow, he would then continue with an angioplasty. During that procedure, a thin catheter with a balloon at its tip would be threaded back up to the plaque-filled artery. The balloon would then be inflated, compressing the plaque against the artery wall and restoring blood flow through the artery. He may additionally decide to place a small, wire-mesh tube called a stent to help permanently prop the artery open, decreasing the chance of it narrowing again.

If Dr. S should find it necessary to perform an angioplasty, I would most likely stay one night in the hospital to ensure there were no complications. On the other hand, if he saw no problems with my coronary arteries, he would simply remove the catheter and I would go home later that day. He stressed again that I needed to remain still and tell him immediately if I was in any kind of pain as he performed the delicate procedure. The nurse would continue to observe me throughout the procedure to be certain I was sedated enough to keep me relaxed and still. I was doing well until Dr. S began discussing with his assistants the size of the stents he would need. Although I was relaxed from the drugs, I was aware and certainly lucid enough to realize he had found one or more partially blocked arteries!

While I was lying there, needing to hold still, my mind wandered and concluded that Dana's autopsy might have saved my life. As Dr. S explained what was going to happen next—reinserting the catheter with the balloon on the tip, inflating the balloon to compress the plaque against the artery, and then inserting the stents one at a time—I almost lost control on that table. I honestly have no idea how I managed to stay still, except that I must have had a strong will to survive. At first, the tears just began dripping down the sides of my face. Then I felt the quiet sobs starting to build as I tried to remain still. Luckily, the nurse assessed the situation and quickly gave me more of the Valium-like medication.

The stirring of these uncontrollable emotions had everything to do with me realizing what had brought me to this place on this day. Dana's murder had led to an autopsy where the medical examiner had found severe coronary-artery disease. That information had led Sarah and me to be tested. The results of my heart scan had led me to have this procedure, which may have saved my life. That insight, while I was still lying on the table during the procedure, led me to realize with 100 percent certainty that I would gladly and without reservation have given my life to save my Dana, instead of this reverse situation.

In the end, I needed three stents inserted because I had about 85 percent blockage in one of my most important coronary arteries. Dr. S came to see us in the recovery area to explain everything he had done and why it had been necessary. Patiently and compassionately, he answered our questions and showed us a photo of my clogged artery before and then the nicely opened artery after the angioplasty and stent insertions. The only nagging question was why I had had no symptoms. How would I know if this was happening again later? This question would wait until my follow-up appointment with my own cardiologist, Dr. L. But for now, I would be good to go home after a watchful night in the hospital.

While in recovery later, when I was alone, I contemplated, *What does God want from me? Why am I still alive and my baby girl is dead? He must have some plan for me that I haven't figured out yet.* These questions required some reflection to come to terms with why I had been given another chance to live but Dana had to die. What I came to understand and eventually accept was that I would never have a complete answer. But I would continue to search for the meaning of why I had been left here and what God wanted from me.

I did not grasp the significance back then, but this health crisis and my ensuing questions caused a dramatic, transformative moment in my faith life. Indeed, it was another moment of grace to help me slowly heal from my broken spirit and my broken heart. Since I would never get an answer as to why I had lived and Dana had died, I vowed to find ways to honor Dana's memory by striving to make a difference in this world in her name. Now I just needed time to begin healing physically and, more importantly, emotionally to figure out where to start.

CHAPTER 11

ONE DAY AT A TIME

> *It is true that grief is a journey, often perilous and without clear direction, one that demands to be taken. Sometimes it begins quietly . . . But more often, grief begins cruelly . . . To whatever degree you grieve, the emotional invasion is inevitable; the feelings are valid and real. . . You can fight them, or you can live through them.*
>
> —Molly Fumia

Without a doubt, as I write my story, my single most significant spiritual experience to date was my journey from the deepest depths of despair to the peace and healing I feel today. I do not remember much about those first several weeks after our lives were changed forever. I am sure Sarah, Joe, and I were each struggling in our own way to make sense of what had happened and why, as well as subconsciously redefining what our new normal would be without Dana. I cannot speak for Joe or Sarah, but I was constantly questioning how I would survive this tragedy and if I could ever be happy again. I struggled often with my unbearable, intense anguish of knowing Dana had died and I had lived. How could I ever accept that unfair reality? Even in my broken emotional state though, without conscious thought, I had begun to define what I needed to heal, right from the beginning, and I continued that process daily.

What resources did I use early on to help me escape from my never-ending thoughts and questions as well as from the mental imagery of the crime? Even from the first day, without being fully conscious of my actions, I began making simple decisions, giving myself permission to make choices that would bring me some comfort and solace. These choices helped me find fleeting moments of peace from the conflicting turmoil of emotions within me: I had made the distress call to Rita and then accepted her invitation to come to Sarah's place when we heard the news of Dana's murder, I had decided I needed to identify Dana at the Cook County Morgue, I had made sure my family would have ample time to arrive for the visitation and funeral mass, I had insisted on a private viewing for Sarah and me as well as other family members, I had taken the time to make the photo boards and the video for the visitation, and I had never stopped the dialogue between Sarah and me as well as the sharing of our pain and sorrow. These were actions over which I had some control and which brought me some moments of comfort amidst the turbulence within my soul. But they were also choices I made to face the pain head on and walk through the fire rather than shying away or drugging myself to numbness. In pain, I was beginning to forge my path to find healing. As the days and weeks went on, I began listening to beautiful, soothing music, reading self-help books on grief, praying often, attending psychotherapy sessions, crying, spending time with friends, and finding ways to keep Dana's memory alive. I discovered quickly what worked for me. All these life-renewing activities helped refresh my spirit and soothe my soul when I most needed that. And so, I returned to one or more of these activities whenever I had a bad day. My healing journey had begun.

I had a collection of music I listened to every night to help me sleep. At first I played a few of the most beautiful songs from the funeral Mass over and over, or an album of sounds of the sea that soothed my exhausted body and spirit. I listened to the music in the car whenever I needed to be consoled, and I listened to it any time I felt lost, alone, scared, or had no idea of how to continue functioning. Eventually this music became a collection of church songs that deeply moved me as well as popular music that did the same. I continually added to my collection and still do to this day. Now, the playlist is a bit different, but soothing, grounding, and comforting nonetheless.

Reawakening

At the funeral luncheon, Rita had given Sarah, Joe, and me our own copies of what became one of my most treasured books, *Safe Passage: Words to Help the Grieving* by Molly Fumia. The author's meditations resonated so strongly with me, as she had put into words so much of what I was feeling. This book became my Bible, so to speak, on my own unique journey toward peace and healing. Because I found comfort and hope for healing in these meditations, I continued to search for other grief-resource books to add to my library. As time passed, I had accumulated quite a wonderful collection. I always loved to share these books of healing with Sarah and Joe. To this day, I occasionally reread sections of the books and use them as resources when needed.

Sarah had stayed with us for the first two weeks until she felt strong enough to return to her condominium in the city. She had not been home for long when she decided she could not yet stay alone. Sarah returned to our house, her safe haven, and stayed for another two or three weeks. Eventually she went back to her own home, trying to settle into a work routine and live her life again.

Joe and I have always grieved very differently. I have found comfort and healing through talking with those special people in my life who can be there with me and for me emotionally, to grieve and cry with me, to journey with me through our life crises, and share our joys as well as our sorrows. Joe's way of dealing with grief is much more private. He prays and communicates with countless Catholic priests, brothers, and nuns through letters and phone calls and relies on their spiritual guidance. He might also have other friends to confide in, but I was not privy to that information.

Sadly, in these weeks since Dana had died, when I attempted to share with Joe how I felt and how much I was grieving early on, he clearly did not want to get involved in those painful conversations with me. And even though I tried several times to engage him in sharing some of his grief with me so we could grieve together, he just could not go to that place. After trying multiple times and getting no response, I simply stopped attempting to connect with my husband on a deep emotional level.

For me, finally being home alone with Joe in our big, empty house was painful indeed. Now that Sarah was back in her own place, Joe and I hardly ever spoke to each other about anything personal or meaningful. I certainly do not recall him ever just coming to me to talk or let us comfort each other. We were like acquaintances, talking about the weather and sports. Not only had I lost my daughter and was struggling with the aftermath of her brutal murder, Joe and I could not even talk about her. So to me, it was like she had never existed. I knew Joe was sharing with others, to some extent, and I resented that. I had no idea what to do about this horribly uncomfortable living situation.

There was one thing I had always taken comfort in, no matter what challenges I faced throughout my life, and that was prayer. And so, I prayed incessantly. In this ancient ritual of praying I knew I would find refuge, peace, and consolation. I prayed for Sarah, for myself, for Joe and our marriage, and for Dana. I prayed in thanksgiving, in sorrow, in confusion, in questioning. I prayed for my Sarah's well-being as I witnessed her intense sorrow and grief, crushed by losing her only sibling and all their shared dreams for the future. I prayed for the wisdom to guide her back to living her life. On another level, because of this selfish act, this heinous crime, my fear of losing my loving, caring, beautiful daughter Sarah was sometimes so intense that, when I went to that place, I could not breathe. In those times, I prayed I would not have to live to lose her too. I prayed in anguish as I realized how alone I felt. I seemed to be invisible in Joe's world of pain and sorrow. I prayed in thanksgiving and gratitude for all of those "sisters at heart"—and for my daughter, Sarah—who were there for me, who were okay to cry with me, laugh with me, and grieve along with me. This was the compassionate and loving gift these beautiful women gave to me, through the Spirit.

My psychological therapy with Rita intensified. I do not know how I would have coped with Dana's murder had Rita not been my therapist. For several months, I met with her at least twice a week. The appointments gradually tapered off as I became stronger. It was a painstakingly slow process, yet one that was critical to my healing. The opportunity to talk with Rita—to have her listen and guide me through my pain, my sorrow, my fears and anxieties, my anger, my relationship issues, and my need to be an active participant in the court process—was exactly what my broken spirit and broken heart craved. She was the one person with whom I could be completely open, trusting that I would not be judged no matter what I said or how I felt. Rita calmly guided me as I struggled to make sense of my life now, without my Dana.

She offered no magic wand to take away my unbearable sorrow; she had no answers for a quick cure. How I would have desperately grabbed for that cure! Her gift, as my therapist, was to listen, to gently question me, to allow me time to work through my wide range of ever-conflicting emotions, and to offer suggestions about resources available to help me along my journey of grief. I already knew, from my years of psychotherapy with Rita, each of us has control over how we live our experiences. I also understood completely that I must not stifle my emotions; I needed to feel them fully, no matter how painful, to reach a place where I could truly live my life again. I had done this work before with Rita, but this time I did not know if I would find my way again. However, I continued my sessions with her. I felt dead inside. I did not want to live like this. From somewhere deep within, I accepted that I must draw again from my inner strength and find the courage necessary to begin a new life for myself, to define my new normal.

Rita helped me as I struggled with my gripping fear of losing Sarah and what that would do to me. It was unhealthy for me to obsess about Sarah's safety when she was out of my sight. If I was not able to control my own demons, how was I helping her in attempting to control her fears and anxieties? As it was, I was trying so hard to remain calm as I watched my daughter become almost paralyzed from the intensity of her own fears, the fear of someone murdering her, and her fear of losing Joe or me. It is not surprising that each of us was so overprotective of the others. Our world had come crashing down in an instant with Dana's brutal murder. Rita and I had much work to do because of my overwhelming fear of losing Sarah too. Only with the passing of time, the power of healing, and my acceptance that Sarah's safety was not under my control did I let go of my obsessive need to hear from her daily.

Rita listened as I grappled with what I saw as the disintegration of my marriage. What I was not aware of at the time was that a large percentage of married couples have serious relationship problems after their child dies. I was certainly experiencing grave doubts as to whether our marriage would survive losing our daughter. What would be the outcome? It was scary to even think about that.

Rita was my sounding board as I obsessed about my need to get answers to why and how this horrible event happened. I had an intense desire to walk with Dana through what had happened, just like I had always walked through my daughters' life journeys with them. There were those in my family and among my friends who could not understand why I needed this information. I knew their intentions were good; they were simply trying to protect me as they questioned why I would want to be hurt repeatedly when I heard the answers. But this choice I made, which I now feel was crucial for my healing, was clearly one example of staying true to myself, even though others tried to dissuade me.

I would highly recommend therapy for anyone who believes they are in too much pain to ever be healed, or thinks a therapist can never understand the grief they are going through, or believes therapy cannot help them. I am not going to lie; therapy can be hard work, but it is also powerfully cathartic if you are honest with yourself and your therapist. If you are finding that nothing is helping you move beyond your pain and sorrow, working with a therapist could become an integral part of your healing process—if you are committed to giving it a chance.

For me to survive this unimaginable tragedy, one thing I was very clear about was that I needed to talk about Dana and to keep her memory alive. We started immediately when we requested in the obituary that any donations in Dana's memory be sent to two organizations that worked for causes close to Dana's heart, as well as to Sarah's and mine. An abundance of generous donations almost immediately poured in to the Anti-Cruelty Society of Chicago and to the Susan G. Komen Breast Cancer Foundation. My heart was filled with gratitude for the remarkable generosity of family members, friends, and neighbors who lovingly contributed, and I found joy even in the midst of deep sorrow because together we were all helping to keep Dana's memory alive.

In September 2007, two of Dana's girlfriends organized a team called The Mooseketeers—named after Dana's beloved dog, Moose—to participate in the PAWS (Pets Are Worth Saving) Chicago run/walk to raise money in Dana's memory for her love of animals. Our team consisted of family, friends, acquaintances, and our mascot, Moose. That inaugural year, just six weeks after Dana died, our team numbered over one hundred people! We won first place in the team category for money raised, over $15,000! I was overcome with emotion when I arrived at the event. We were all meeting to get a group photograph of our team. As soon as we arrived, Sarah, Joe, and I were drawn into this wonderful group of people, all here for us and for Dana, to show their love, compassion, and support for us. I rode an emotional roller coaster that morning between experiencing incredible sadness for why we were here in the first place and surprising joy because we were doing something so special; we were collectively raising money for dogs and cats in Dana's memory. Our team, The Mooseketeers, has continued to participate in this wonderful event every year since 2007.

CHAPTER 12

SALT IN THE WOUND

The very act of struggling to breathe when grief has deprived you of air is a sign of your spirit stirring. Even as the heart is breaking, the pieces begin to inch back. Even though the little things bring sobs up to your throat, and confusion has crushed any sense of normalcy in your life, something within you is plotting survival.

—Molly Fumia

At the end of September 2007, Joe, Sarah, and I flew to Minneapolis with heavy hearts. We dreaded the task that awaited us: clearing out the condominium Dana had rented a few months earlier. It was unfathomable to me that, only a few months ago, Joe and I had helped Dana move in and unpack, sharing her nervousness of starting a new life and her excitement about starting veterinary school. What a bright future lay ahead for my daughter! I had looked forward with excited anticipation to sharing the journey with her. Instead, here we were, broken and burdened with the horrible task of dismantling Dana's life and her dreams. Our plan was that Joe, Sarah, and I would pack up the condo and clean it on Friday and Saturday. On Sunday morning, the movers would be there to load a rental truck with whatever we decided to bring home.

Physically and emotionally exhausted after a delayed flight into Minneapolis, we drove to our hotel in the early morning hours and went to sleep. The three of us got to work Friday morning right after breakfast. Our hotel was conveniently located right across the street from the condominium complex. The last time I had been at Dana's Minneapolis home, she and I had finished unpacking most of her things. The condo had begun to take shape and look like a home. For me, walking into Dana's place with Joe and Sarah and seeing Dana's home as she had decorated it, putting her personality into this comfortable space, pierced my broken heart once again. In my fragile emotional state, the tears could not be contained. How could I do what needed to be done here in just three days? I felt like an intruder as I stepped into Dana's life; she had left her place certainly planning on returning soon. A University of Minnesota fleece jacket (that Joe had bought her) hung over a chair in the kitchen, mail was on the kitchen counter, notes were posted on a small bulletin board, messages were on Dana's answering machine, her toiletries were sitting on her bathroom sink, food items were in her cabinets and in the refrigerator. Her pretty little home had a lived-in look. I did not want to take it apart bit by bit, but that was the daunting task before us.

This overwhelming amount of work needed to be organized in just a couple of days. We would collectively decide what we wanted to keep, what we would give away, and what we would be willing to throw away. In the best-case scenario, this enormous undertaking would be challenging to complete in a few days. But we were in the throes of grieving and trying to make sense of what had happened. Stepping into her life was a heart-wrenching reminder that Dana was lost to us forever.

We would not be without reinforcements, however. My youngest brother and our nephew would fly up to Minneapolis on Saturday late afternoon. The two of them would help us on Saturday and early Sunday, if necessary, with any last-minute packing. Then they would drive the rental truck back to Chicago on Sunday. Joe, Sarah, and I would fly home after they left and meet them back at our house eventually that Sunday to unpack the truck.

In the meantime, once the three of us arrived at Dana's place that Friday morning, we made an initial assessment of the job ahead of us before we threw ourselves into sorting and packing. I had allowed myself a short time to emotionally process my feelings, and then did as I had often done in the past—I slipped into autopilot to function somewhat normally and get the packing done. Sarah and I thought it best to give Joe the task of unhooking and packing all the electronics. We both sensed he would not handle sorting Dana's clothes, shoes, linens, school stuff, and personal items well.

Sarah and I left Joe downstairs as we headed upstairs to Dana's bedroom. Emptying each dresser drawer, we sorted things into four piles: clothes to give away, clothes to throw away, clothes Sarah wanted to keep, and those items that held a special meaning to me. Next, we attacked her walk-in closet. Certainly, at times we cried and at times we laughed as we shared memories that popped into our heads. At one point, we were sorting through Dana's large shoe collection. She had several pairs of shoes and boots that Sarah wanted to keep. I felt like I was watching one of Cinderella's stepsisters trying to force her feet into shoes that were obviously too small. I started giggling as Sarah tried shoving her feet into the boots and shoes, to no avail. She had to grudgingly admit someone else was going to be the lucky recipient of those items. I still chuckle when I think about that scene and have shared it on occasion. We were given a little gift of humor in a heartbreaking situation.

Eventually Joe's curiosity got the best of him, so when he appeared in the doorway and saw our various piles, he asked why we were not going to give all the clothes away or throw them away. Why would we spend valuable time sorting? He said we would not have enough room in the truck for all Dana's "junk." I think he realized quickly there was no chance he was going to win that battle as he walked out, seeming quite annoyed with the time and effort we were putting into this task. I was not even aware enough to verbalize my feelings, but I know now I needed more time to let go of much of the stuff I had brought home. Thinking back on that scenario, I believe Joe's swift reaction was because seeing all of Dana's stuff would remind him of her and cause him deep pain, which he was trying to avoid. Interestingly, he did give Sarah the University of Minnesota fleece jacket, and he also took Dana's lanyard from her job at the university's veterinary clinic. I had never even seen the lanyard or known he had kept it until I learned about it months later.

After a long day of sorting and packing, the three of us had dinner. Before settling in for the night at our hotel, Sarah and I were drawn back to Dana's place. Because of our limited time frame, the day had been terribly hectic. I trusted that both Sarah and I craved some quiet time at Dana's home, to be with her spirit there before the place was dismantled the next day. Joe returned to our hotel room. Sarah and I lay together in Dana's bed, holding each other, sometimes crying, sometimes talking, and sometimes silent while lost in our own individual reflections and memories. We had been so busy that entire day that we had not been quiet long enough to let our grief in and truly feel Dana's spirit here with us. The merciful and compassionate God I believe in was with Sarah and me that evening, enfolding us in His loving arms and comforting us as we opened ourselves to feel our sorrow and our pain.

Each time I did what I felt was best for me, each time I allowed myself to feel the unbearable pain and walk through it, was another tiny step in the long healing process of my heart and my soul. I was grateful Sarah was able to do the same. Even back then, I was certain that avoiding feelings (denial, despair, anger, pain, sorrow, guilt), fighting them instead of living through them, was unhealthy both emotionally and physically. I worried about Joe's physical and emotional well-being, even as I struggled with my own anger toward him for not allowing me to share his pain and suffering. But I was in a fight for my own life, my own emotional and physical well-being, and I did not have the energy or the desire to put much effort into trying to help him at this time in my journey.

The staff of the veterinary school had arranged a tour for us and a meeting time to visit with an advisor who would help us set up a scholarship fund in Dana's memory. So, the following day, Sarah and I took a break to drive over to the University of Minnesota College of Veterinary Medicine campus. Our first stop, though, was to head over to the pharmacy to meet Dana's coworkers, the doctors and the staff with whom she had worked for several weeks before returning home in August. We were welcomed with such kindness and compassion from these strangers. My heart was filled with gratitude as they each shared their experiences in getting to know Dana. She had endeared herself to them with her excitement about attending veterinary school, with her "spunk" and her beautiful smile, and with her stories and pictures of our family and our pets that left such an impression on them, even in the little time they had known her. I sensed almost immediately why Dana had loved her job there as well as the people with whom she worked, and why she had felt a sense of belonging to this vet-school family.

After thanking the pharmacy staff for giving us the chance to meet them and see where Dana had worked, we said our goodbyes. Then, as we were guided on our own private tour of the College of Veterinary Medicine, I was awed by the technology available to these aspiring veterinary students. We wandered through the halls—through student labs, classrooms, diagnostic testing facilities, surgery and recovery rooms, and so much more. Sorrow washed over me as I pictured Dana here in these corridors, in these classrooms, and I was filled with sadness because my opportunity to walk this amazing journey with her had been cruelly stolen from me. On the other hand, it was such a special gift for Sarah and me to be given the chance to explore this place where Dana's life would have continued. After that tour ended, we met with a few individuals who explained the process of creating a memorial scholarship fund in Dana's memory. We certainly wanted to pursue this opportunity and left that meeting with information about scholarships and the next steps in the process. My initial impression during Dana's interview weekend, that this College of Veterinary Medicine was a place with a strong sense of community and respect among students and faculty, was only enhanced by our experience this day. Each person we met was so gracious, kind, and welcoming. I now understood more clearly why I had felt that Dana would be comfortable here and accepted into this community. Through Dana, I will always feel a special connection to this place.

Back at the condominium, the three of us finished packing later that afternoon. Unbelievably, we were organized and ready for the moving company to load our rental truck the next day. By now, my brother and our nephew had arrived, and after we all went to dinner Saturday night, we brought them over to see the condo before all returning to our rooms. Sarah and I were drawn back to Dana's place once again, but it no longer looked like Dana's home. It felt sterile, sanitized, devoid of her spirit. The downstairs was filled with boxes and bags as well as furniture. There was nothing left up in her bedroom but her stripped bed and the dressers. Filled with intense sorrow and overflowing emotions, we left this depressing reminder of a life dismantled.

Sunday morning the movers arrived to pack the truck. The same young men who had unloaded the truck almost three months earlier remembered us. They did not ask why we were moving her stuff again and we did not share that information. Dana's condo was a beehive of activity that morning and early afternoon. While the movers were busy with the heavy items, some of our friends from St. Cloud, Minnesota, showed up amid the chaos. They had agreed to stop by with their SUV because I had been unsuccessful in finding any local charity organizations that would pick up the furniture we wanted to give away. These dear friends were so kind to take the items we wanted to donate and find charities in and around St. Cloud. Amazingly, they fit a big love seat, several other pieces of furniture, and many bags of clothes and shoes in their vehicle with the help of Joe and the guys.

While I was directing everyone, Sarah disappeared upstairs at some point to be alone. It was there my girlfriend found her in a corner of Dana's empty bedroom, despondent and crying, and tried to comfort and console her. I did not know this until days later when my friend shared it with me. My broken heart was pierced again at the image of my beautiful, broken Sarah, alone and in such pain. Thank God my girlfriend had been there for her.

Once the truck was loaded and our St. Cloud friends were on their way home, we said goodbye to our relatives as they began the long drive back to our house in the Chicago suburbs. If everything went as planned, we would be home by the time they arrived with the truck. After all paperwork was completed and Dana's keys were turned in, back we went to the airport for our flight home. As our plane took off and I saw the cities of Minneapolis and St. Paul below, I started crying as I realized the finality of the situation. Dana's life, as we knew it, had been packed away, given away, and thrown away. There was no place I could go anymore that was truly hers. Her bedroom at our house, after our renovation in 2005, was simply filled with a bed, dressers, and some lamps since she had moved out several years before. It was also devoid of her spirit and energy, but it was all I had.

On the flight home, I began journaling to express my thoughts and feelings. Rita had suggested this as a powerful tool to add to my arsenal of healing resources. Most importantly, I could write without censoring as I poured out my heart and soul on paper. I quickly discovered that this personal and private journal of mine was unconditionally accepting and nonjudgmental. Any time I felt all jumbled up inside, or angry, or unsure of what I wanted or what I was feeling and why, I could simply jot down my thoughts and emotions without any sort of editing. What an insightful way to help me get in touch with my inner self, uncensored! Sometimes when I reread sections of my journal from those first few years, I still wonder about the miracle of my journey from those days of agony and despair to where I am now. My journaling was crucial to my healing, so I believe strongly that journaling can be a powerful tool for helping people going through the grieving process.

CHAPTER 13

NOW WHAT DO I DO?

Once home from Minnesota, I was like a whirling dervish going through all the bags and boxes we brought home, sorting what other items I thought Sarah might want and what I wanted to keep. There had been so much "stuff" we were unable to let go of easily in Minneapolis, but now I had the time to decide what I wanted to save. I became obsessed with going through everything. Our basement floor was covered with multiple piles. Eventually the enormity of the task overwhelmed me to the extent that I had neither the physical nor emotional energy to move forward. As a result, the basement was left a complete mess for months. I could not bring myself to return to the task for quite some time.

Dana's bedroom became another dumping ground for certain things I decided to hold on to, those items that held a special place in my heart. But more importantly, it became my safe haven anytime sleep eluded me at night. I would curl up in Dana's bed and feel as if she were there, close to me. Here I could cry, remember, meditate, and listen to my music, as well as toss and turn without disrupting Joe's sleep.

My strong desire to find out why Dana had been murdered continued. It was still early in the investigation. Of course, I did not learn much because there were no answers for me. How was I going to come to terms with what had happened to Dana if I never got an answer? In my quest to find some closure, I had to do some soul searching—why did I feel such an intense desire to get information? This was my daughter; I had to know because I am her mom. I had always been her protector. I had tried to guide her throughout her life, and I had comforted her when she was hurt. I was tormented imagining her scared and hurt, knowing I had not been there for her or with her. I prayed she had gone to a place where she was remembering how much we all loved her and where she was with God. Maybe by walking through this nightmare, by being there as Dana's advocate, I could put to rest this anguish I carried.

Would I be able to deal with the horrible images and nightmares if what I learned was more than I could handle? As difficult as it might be to find out the gruesome details, I realized I had such horrifying pictures in my head imagining the scenario. Knowing the truth might help erase some of my most atrocious images. That had been the case when I had identified Dana's body at the Cook County Morgue. Based on that experience, I reasoned, for me, it would be beneficial to learn more of the facts. Scarily, though, since Joe did not want to know anything, I realized whatever I was told might be my burden to bear alone. Therefore, I needed to take baby steps.

During this dark period, these first few months after Dana's death, as I was sorting through so many feelings, thoughts, doubts, and memories, I persisted in painstakingly defining what I needed to do for myself regardless of what others thought. And I continued to fight for what I needed, including insisting Joe and I visit a therapist together who specialized in helping couples who have lost a child. In my opinion, our uneasy, awkward living situation had not improved in the least. At the beginning of this nightmare, I had tried hard to respect our differences, to allow Joe to deal with Dana's murder in his own way and me to deal with it in mine. But before too long, I felt I was being forced to give in to Joe's need to grieve in private, because I believed I was being shut out of his life. I so desperately wanted to feel an emotional connection with Joe in our loss, but I did not experience that at all. So, I prayed for guidance as we began couples therapy—as I wondered if our marriage would survive, or if I even wanted it to survive.

As Joe and I walked this journey together, yet alone, I experienced futility as well as rejection, anger, sorrow, vulnerability, and abandonment. As I struggled alone in the seemingly bottomless abyss of my anguish and despair, I thought couples therapy might be our last chance. I could not imagine continuing to live with someone with whom I felt no emotional connection. That realization scared the hell out of me. There was a huge elephant in the room at our house, and I believed our marriage was dying a slow and painful death. "The Elephant in the Room" by Terry Kettering is a poem that brought me to tears when I read it in these early days after Dana died. The elephant in the room for me was that Joe and I could not talk about Dana at all, not about her life, her horrendous death, or the pain and sorrow we were both experiencing, each on our own but never together. I wanted to talk about more than just trivial matters, the weather, sports, or our jobs. We talked about everything except anything to do with Dana. Her death had crushed both of us, but my feeling was if we could only talk about her death, then maybe we could eventually also talk about her life as well as our memories of Dana. And if we could not get there, I would be left alone with the huge elephant in the room.

At home, I never did have the conversation with Joe that I thought our marriage was dying a slow death, or that I was seriously questioning if I could stay in our marriage when I felt no emotional connection with him. Since I could not break through his wall at all, I did not have the strength or will to even broach this subject with him. I had known and accepted for a long time that no one person can meet all our needs. In my deep pain, however, I could not see past my strong desire to have a husband who could share this horrific nightmare with me, one who could share his vulnerability with me and let me share my vulnerability with him.

When Joe and I began our couples therapy sessions, it was in Dr. F's office that we talked about our differences in grieving. I have always found comfort and healing in talking with those I can trust who will listen, who will not judge or try to fix things, who will not get uncomfortable and tell me I shouldn't feel a certain way, who will not silence me by quickly telling me things will get better. These special angels have always had the capacity to simply be present with me, sharing in my raw pain and sorrow, crying, and laughing with me. I shared with Dr. F and Joe, early on, my perspective of Joe's much more private way of dealing with his grief, his communicating with priests, brothers, and nuns through letters and calls. Other than sharing with those individuals, I had absolutely no idea how he was coping with his grief or, for that matter, how he was feeling.

As our therapy continued and we all got to know each other a little better, Dr. F started by asking each of us how we were doing. Joe usually deferred to me to begin. I remember sharing that I felt like I was doing well in my healing journey as I constantly focused on my life-renewing activities every chance I got. But as a couple, I stated I did not think we were doing well at all. I shared with them that the only time I had learned anything personal about Joe's grief journey was actually during our sessions with Dr. F, and I was so relieved when Joe would share even a small piece of himself. It was in one of these sessions I learned Joe had kept Dana's lanyard from the University of Minnesota in his desk drawer at home. He had finally been brave enough to wear it to work one day, and many of his work colleagues commented on how wonderful it was that he had her lanyard. I expressed, even though I never doubted Joe was suffering, how powerful it was for me to finally hear out loud these little details about Joe's grief journey. I thought this would be a breakthrough session for Joe and me to slowly heal together. Sadly, though, at home we just could not find common ground.

This same situation happened more than once in Dr. F's office. Therefore, not surprisingly, I was increasingly resentful that Joe would not freely share this same information with me outside of the therapist's office. In these sessions, I expressed my frustration, my resentfulness, and my sadness about Joe only sharing his grief journey with me when we were with Dr. F. But nothing I said or did made any difference in repairing what I saw as the huge rift in our emotional relationship. Reflecting on those months with Dr. F, I believe Joe was just not willing or able to break down his wall and let me in. Even when we were in Dr. F's office, I saw no progress in sparking any kind of emotional connection. Therefore, I had no interest in bringing up the more serious topic of my belief that our marriage was dying a slow death and that I felt I had no emotional connection with Joe, much less asking what Joe thought about the status of our marriage. My own pain and suffering from losing Dana was exacerbated now by my perception that I had also lost my husband. To me, he seemed just a shell of a man, someone I no longer knew at all other than in a superficial way.

I had been working hard with Rita for quite some time to express my feelings, wants, and needs more clearly to my husband. And, before Dana died, I had been much more confident in being able to express myself in a healthy way and continue to have a voice in my relationship with Joe. I was happier and more content in my marriage than I had been in years. However, on that worst day of my life, when Joe had seemed to shut down and shut me out of anything he was feeling, it had been impossible for me to refrain from falling back into my unhealthy habit of keeping my emotions in check when I was under that much stress myself. From my perspective, I believe Dana's death and the ensuing emotional disconnect between Joe and me was the spark that ignited what I felt was the deterioration of my marriage. We were each distraught, and our emotional shutdowns mirrored each other. Accepting what I needed, and not expecting Joe to help me, was so important for me to realize. However, it would be many months before I came to that healing place.

Unfortunately for us, Dr. F retired after we had been seeing him for several months. Although I would miss his guidance and support, I did take away an important lesson from our sessions with him. Since I had learned most of what I now knew about Joe's healing process in these sessions, I did not believe that with Dr. F we had gotten much closer to working through our issues as a couple. The chasm between Joe and me was not going to be bridged anytime soon. Truthfully, I did not have the energy to even pursue further counseling with a different therapist. However, if Joe had expressed interest in continuing with someone else, I most definitely would have tried to find a different therapist. But he never did so. All I could hope for was to continue my healing journey in as healthy a way as possible. That must be my focus.

CHAPTER 14

THE FIRST HOLIDAYS LOOM

Running from my grief, I am not silent or still long enough to let it in. But the fullness of existence is facing both life and death, and taking the risks involved in that confrontation. To have loved you is to have opened up to a willingness to feel your loss. This is the time of reckoning. I must stop to feel my sorrow.

—Molly Fumia

As a mother who had buried her child just a few months earlier, the dreaded "firsts" loomed in my mind as Thanksgiving and Christmas approached. We had been hosting these two holidays for many years already, and I always looked forward to our traditional dinners and spending time with Joe's small extended family. But as the days approached, I realized I had no energy nor desire to spend Thanksgiving or Christmas in our home that year. Grief and sorrow had ripped from me the joy and happiness of the holiday celebrations fast approaching. The thought of celebrating here in our house and trying to enjoy all our holiday traditions without Dana was more than I could bear. On the other hand, I wanted to do something small for these upcoming holidays. Sarah, Joe, and I needed to define what was best for us since we all agreed it was just too painful to host Thanksgiving or Christmas in 2007.

I did struggle a bit about this decision, however. I knew our extended family was also suffering, and I was confident they would find comfort in all of us being together. Yet I could not even imagine spending these holidays at one of their houses either, because wherever we all were together, the memories of sharing celebrations with Dana would be too intense. However, family has always been so important to me, and I did not want to hurt them even more than they were already hurting. With that in mind, Joe and I planned that for Thanksgiving we would spend several nights in downtown Chicago at a hotel close to Sarah's small condominium. We invited our small family to share a turkey dinner with us at a Chicago restaurant on Thanksgiving Day. As for our first Christmas without Dana, we chose to get away from our hometown and all the memories of past Christmases at our house. Joe, Sarah, and I decided to spend three nights at a resort in Galena, Illinois. Once those plans were finalized and I had discussed all this with my sisters-in-law and our niece and nephew, I found some peace with our decisions. Having been the hostess for many years, I had been able to lower my expectations and eliminate the pressure I put on myself to celebrate the way we always did.

At the same time as I was starting to think about what Sarah, Joe, and I might do for Thanksgiving and Christmas, I had been in contact with Mike, the prosecutor on Dana's murder case, as I had begun to ask questions to try to understand why Dana had been murdered. As Thanksgiving 2007 drew near, I scheduled a meeting with Mike and with our victim specialist. A victim specialist assists victims and/or their families during the criminal justice process, providing support and helping them prepare for the courtroom experience. Our victim specialist, Pam, had been assigned to be with our family whenever we were in court. Sarah had decided to go with me to this first meeting on the day before Thanksgiving. As I have already mentioned, I had realized early on that I needed to know as much as possible about what had happened to my younger daughter. I had walked with Dana her entire life, and I needed to be there for her and with her through this entire process, no matter what the outcome would be. I prayed often that my God would take care of my fragile emotional state as I began this unreal journey through the court system.

As I was on my way to the Criminal Court Building of Cook County, I realized this was a day that could either quell my most horrible imaginings or add to them. Although I was fearful about what answers I might find, I was also confident in the knowledge this was what I needed to do for myself. Even so, I was not nearly as confident Sarah would be ready to hear the answers to some of the questions I wanted to ask: Did he say why he killed her? What did he do to her, that we know of, while she was still alive and after she was dead? Why did he stab her after he strangled her? The last thing I wanted to do was cause her any more pain or heartbreak. But she wanted to come with me and I could not tell her no, nor make her decisions for her. However, I did review with Sarah my list of questions so she could be prepared to leave the room, if necessary. And then I placed myself in the loving and comforting arms of my God, asking Him to take care of me and of Sarah in this endeavor. I hoped and prayed this day that, when we met with our team, we would both be able to handle the answers to whatever questions I asked. When I left that in God's hands, He answered that prayer for me and, I believe, for Sarah. In gratitude for their honesty, compassion, and respect for us, we thanked Mike and Pam and headed back into downtown Chicago, where I would meet Joe at our hotel.

I was definitely not yet ready to show up in court to face Dana's murderer after that first meeting with the lead prosecutor on her case. But what I had realized that day, after leaving Mike's office, was that I now had two wonderful advocates who would walk with me through my journey in the court system. What a powerful realization for me that, even if in the future I went to court by myself, I would not be alone. In the months after that initial meeting, occasionally I contacted Mike by phone with more questions. The court hearings had been going on for several months already, and I knew myself well enough that at some point I would inform Mike I was ready to come to court.

For me, Thanksgiving has been a day to reflect on all the blessings bestowed on me as well as on those I love, to attend a morning Mass to give thanks for all my blessings, and to celebrate a meal with family. This year would certainly not follow our traditional pattern. We had planned on keeping it simple. It offered Joe, Sarah, and me plenty of downtime, and still included Joe's family. I craved time alone to grieve and reflect on my memories without the distraction of social obligations, time to pray in a quiet space and to attempt to reflect on my blessings. Thanksgiving afternoon, we met Joe's two sisters as well as our nephew at the restaurant. It was with heavy hearts that we gathered to share this meal together.

As I had vowed to always find ways to honor Dana's memory, I had an idea earlier in the week that I would ask each person at our table to share some special memory they had experienced with Dana. There was certainly no lack of funny or tender stories to share. I hoped that in this way she would be there with us in spirit and we might be able to smile or even laugh at some of the stories. As it turned out, a few of us were able to verbalize an endearing memory. For the others, I sensed it was too painful to think about. One funny story, though, made us all chuckle: when clearing away the dirty dishes from our holiday dinners, we always knew where Dana had been seated by the number of spills and crumbs around her plate. One thing was clear—she had always eaten with gusto!

Weirdly, even though I had made the reservation for six people, there ended up being an empty chair at our table that day. The significance was not lost on us, as we thought about Dana and commented that she *was* there with us in spirit at this somber Thanksgiving dinner. After dinner Sarah, Joe, and I said our goodbyes to the family. For the rest of the weekend, we spent time together and time alone as we each simply attempted to get through the remainder of the holiday weekend the best that we could.

Christmas, for me, is a special, holy day. As much as Thanksgiving is a day to give thanks for all we have been blessed with, Christmas is so much more than that. Don't get me wrong. Although Christmas is a sacred, holy day, I love the season of Christmas: the decorations, the wonderful Christmas songs and beautiful Christmas church music, giving to those we love and finding opportunities to give to those who are less fortunate than us, the Christmas cookies and candies, and the special family traditions. I too can get caught up in all the commercial hustle and bustle of the season to the extent that it distracts me from the real meaning of Christmas, if I don't make a concerted effort each day for a short time of reflection and prayer. But first and foremost, the Christmas season is about preparing for the birth of the baby Jesus, and Christmas Day is about celebrating God's greatest gift of love to us, the birth of the Christ child.

For much of my daughters' lives, as a family, we attended the Christmas Eve Mass celebrating the birth of Jesus. I loved to hear them sing all the beautiful church music of the Christmas season, with their little girl voices and then with their beautiful young adult voices. When they were little, the three of us would read the Christmas story throughout Advent and then each Christmas Eve before going to church. Eventually they would whisper the Christmas reading of the birth of Jesus along with the priest at Mass. Even as they grew up, it remained our tradition for many years to read the Christmas story before heading off to church. I am confident they always knew the true meaning of Christmas, and that still brings much joy to my heart. Of course, Christmas was delightful as we opened our gifts to each other in the morning and then, later in the day, as we shared our traditional Italian Christmas dinner celebration with Joe's family. That was always a huge success and a great time filled with conversation and laughter.

The Christmas holiday and holy day has a much deeper meaning to me than Thanksgiving, which is most likely why I wanted to remove myself from all our typical traditions on Christmas 2007. As much as I love my church's Christmas Eve Mass, I couldn't bear to be there this year. In addition, I had no energy whatsoever to spend Christmas with anyone but Joe and Sarah. The three of us all agreed this was what we wanted and needed to do for ourselves.

The resort we were staying at was just outside of Galena, Illinois. We had driven there in a blinding snowstorm, praying we would make it as we saw car after car and truck after truck stuck in ditches along the highway. The small town of Galena was basically shut down. Everything was so still, and there was not much going on to keep our minds occupied. We circled the wagons and hunkered down, as each one of us was simply trying to get through this Christmas the best we could. At least we had each other, but the overwhelming loss was palpable. We each retreated into ourselves at times, drowning in our pain and in our despair. At other times, Sarah and I would share our grief and our sorrow, or just spend quiet time together. We all had the luxury of spending time alone or together, watching movies and playing games. On Christmas Eve, we ventured out to attend a Mass at a tiny Catholic church in Galena. Before Mass started, as the choir sang "Silent Night," I started crying and couldn't seem to stop. I couldn't bear the knowledge that we would never again celebrate this special holiday and beautiful holy day with Dana. Eventually I calmed down and was present in this church, even as I realized how much I missed the community of my own church at home. I would be glad to get home after the holidays were over!

Because of the snowstorm, the rolling landscape of the resort property all around us was breathtaking and undisturbed. In the stillness and the serenity of nature, I discovered peace and a sense of closeness to Dana in the beauty of God's creation. What I received from this getaway was the gift of time, which allowed my plethora of emotions to surface. When I needed to spend time alone for reflection, for grieving, or for being in God's healing presence, I would take a short walk in the snow. Holidays have a way of stealing our time. In getting away from our traditional Christmas activities and all the distractions, I was blessed with the gift of uninterrupted time. That opportunity allowed me to fully feel my grief. In my therapy sessions with Rita, I had experienced in powerful ways throughout the years that if I do not ignore the emotional pain, if I can find a way to walk through the pain and allow myself to feel it, I will be able to move on to find a place of true healing. With that knowledge always in the forefront of my thoughts and actions, my healing journey continued as the new year approached.

CHAPTER 15

A NEW YEAR DAWNS

As the new year of 2008 approached, none of us had any intention of celebrating in any fashion. I was driving back to the suburbs from Sarah's house that afternoon of New Year's Eve. As I listened to a favorite song called "In the Quiet" by Liam Lawton, I fell apart and began crying. I had just sung the phrase "leave the past behind and move into the light," and I screamed silently, *NO! I don't want to leave the past behind, I don't want to move into a new year without Dana!* That reaction had just come out of the blue. Nothing prepares you for those unanticipated feelings. This was one of the first of many more I would experience in my grieving and healing process through the years. It was those sudden reactions, the unexpected ones, that would upset my fragile state of being. But as I eventually would come to understand and accept, this was my reality. The most important lesson I took away from these intense and agonizing reactions was that I must always allow myself to walk through the fire of this searing, heart-wrenching pain of the loss of my daughter. In every case, that would help me to move on to continue my healing process, define my new normal, and not stay stuck in the past.

The three of us continued along, each at our own pace and in our own unique way. Sarah and I carried on with our psychological counseling sessions and were able to support, comfort, listen to, and cry with each other, and at times hold each other up. On the other hand, I felt Joe maintained his emotional distance from us, as if it were too painful for him to grieve with us. So, I persisted in forging my own path separate from my husband, as I instinctively knew that was what I needed to do for my own emotional healing.

Joe and I had an opportunity to travel to the island of Great Exuma in the Bahamas in late January of 2008. During the trip, I had an awakening about where I was along my path of healing and how I could find peace and comfort in the beauty all around me. That getaway refreshed my spirit in a way I had never expected. I felt the loving embrace of God in that beautiful place, comforting me and gently leading me to feel alive and happy at times.

Journal entry: January 27, 2008

I'm sitting on a beach in Great Exuma in the Bahamas ... Joe and his boss flew a group of ten people down here 3 days ago. [I had been invited to fly down commercially to enjoy the three days with Joe.] *We go home tomorrow. Sitting down here at the beach of the resort yesterday and today has given me some quiet, undisturbed reflection time. I've been thinking a lot about Dana and where I am in my grieving process. I am proud of all the work I've done up until now ... I feel like there are days when things seem to be better; I have more energy, I get involved, I feel like making the effort in whatever it is that I need to or want to do, I don't dwell as often on her murder, the horror of it, and the frustration of not knowing exactly what happened. I think of her and things about her that make me smile or at least feel good with the memories. I know these are all positive steps in the right direction.*

On the other hand, sometimes I do feel so very guilty for moving on, for not being in that earlier place where I cried so much and felt like a robot as I went through my days. I know that is a part of grieving, feeling survivors' guilt that we are able to be happy and be alive and enjoy life. As Rita told me recently, it is merciful that we do not stay in that other place. It would be too painful to remain in the past and not move on. Some people never move past that early stage of grief ... Rita helped me to see that where I am now is so much more healthy. I will never, ever forget my beautiful daughter, Dana. All the memories of our life together are always there, just under the conscious surface, for me to bring up whenever I want. [This internal struggle, however, would continue off and on amidst the storm of my conflicting feelings. But with Rita's help, I was beginning to accept that it is merciful to get to a place where we can find happiness again.]

Sitting here in this most amazingly beautiful natural setting, I feel the hand of God in this creation. I feel Dana here with me in the soft breeze, in the powerful waves, in the soothing sound of water lapping the shore. I think when I get sad now it's most often about missing her presence — her funny, stubborn, caring personality, about my shattered dreams of a future with her, about sharing her life as she followed her dream of becoming a vet, of finding a soulmate, of having babies. That future has been taken from me.

I love my daughters more than I can ever put into words. I have/had a wonderful relationship with them both. I have no regrets when I think about not being able to have the chance to talk to Dana before she died. [There was nothing I needed to say for closure.] *I have loved her to the best of my ability. I counseled her, taught her about her faith, her values, about being in relationship with others. I protected her, I prodded her on when she needed that, I was a cheerleader to her, I learned to let go (although I fought that sometimes), and I let her make mistakes, fall and pick herself up and move on. I comforted her when she was hurting, I tried (although I don't know how successful I was) to not let her see that my heart was breaking for her when she was hurting. We spent time together laughing and crying, we hugged, we kissed, we expressed our love and our annoyance or anger with each other. And I feel exactly the same about my relationship with Sarah.*

In January 2008, I received a pamphlet about a support group for parents of murdered children (POMC). It piqued my interest, and after doing some research, I was definitely interested in attending one of their meetings. Even though there were no convenient locations near me, I was drawn to this support network, hoping to find comfort, understanding, and support among others who had gone through what I was dealing with. I found that the closest POMC meeting was in Wheaton, Illinois, about a thirty-five-mile drive for me. I was undeterred, and so, on a cold and dark February evening, my sister-in-law Linda and I drove to our first meeting. I did not know exactly what to expect. My emotions were still raw from the pain, heartbreak, and anger of Dana being murdered, and I was not sure I could even talk without breaking down.

The members of this wonderful organization welcomed us with open arms to their select group that no one would willingly join. Everyone there, except one of our coleaders, who was employed by the DuPage County Courthouse, had lost a child, a sibling, a relative, or a friend to violence. From the moment we walked into that room and heard others' stories, I felt a strong connection to these people and a remarkable level of trust unlike anything I had experienced before. Instinctively I knew I could bare my soul and not be judged by whatever I might feel or say about the circumstances of Dana's murder.

My heart was breaking for each person who shared their story with Linda and me. Their bravery and willingness to share their pain and talk about their loved ones who had been murdered gave me the strength to share my story briefly that night. This was a place where I found unconditional acceptance, unparalleled understanding, and overwhelming compassion. I knew I belonged here and I sensed this support group would become an important source of healing for me like no other.

I would encourage anyone who lost a loved one that was murdered, who wishes to find others who can understand what you are experiencing, to attend any type of group like Parents of Murdered Children (POMC). The website for the National Organization of

Parents of Murdered Children, Inc. is pomc.org. They have many chapters throughout the United States. I have no doubt that, for me, attending my POMC group was instrumental in my journey to healing, especially in the early years after Dana died. The benefits of attending this group for me were a safe, welcoming place where I did not have to be afraid to say how I felt; an emotional support system to help me deal with acute grief; and a place where I could come to listen, cry, laugh, and share only as much as I was comfortable sharing without judgment. The healing power of this group for me was that no one could understand exactly what I was dealing with as well as those who were there with me.

Through the years that I have attended POMC, I have been blessed to have developed deep friendships with some of the longtime group participants in a way I had never expected when I decided to attend the first meeting. These dear friends were put in my life when I needed them the most. We have shared our deepest sorrows, our darkest thoughts and feelings, our joys, our healing moments, our fears, our anger, and our frustrations without judgment or ridicule. We have found joy in our friendships and we have shared much laughter, even amidst our pain and loss. I will always cherish this wonderful group of special friends, even as our lives change and group members come and go. I only hope that, throughout the years since I have been a part of this POMC group, I have helped others in their healing journeys in a small way, as they have all helped me.

CHAPTER 16

LIFE GOES ON

Life seemingly continued like normal all around me despite my feeling that life would never be the same. I had returned to work early in 2008 and even though my heart was not in my job, I was making a valiant attempt to resume a more normal schedule. My boss and my coworkers were compassionate and understanding as I tried to find some semblance of order.

Guilt still resurfaced occasionally when I found myself happy and laughing again. Then, suddenly, I would realize I was forgetting the horror of Dana's death and would think to myself, *I shouldn't be happy when my Dana is gone forever*. When I was in that place, I felt like I was a horrible mother to laugh or enjoy myself in any way. But I continued to make use of my arsenal of healing practices, which helped me deal with this survivor's guilt as well as my sorrow and unbearable loss: listening to beautiful, soothing music, reading self-help books dealing with grief, praying often, attending psychotherapy sessions, crying, spending time with friends, journaling, and finding ways to keep Dana's memory alive. These healing tools soothed my troubled heart and soul. In addition, I persisted in searching for any new resources that would help me in my journey.

Support came my way from so many sources. There was the Parents of Murdered Children group who took me under their wing with unconditional love and kindness. Sarah, as well as loving family members and friends, continued to walk this nightmarish journey with me. Our prosecutor, Mike, was always respectful, compassionate, and willing to meet with me when I had more questions and concerns. The lead detective on our case, Detective

Ed, gave me his contact information so I could also call him with questions. And last but certainly not least, I was blessed to have Rita, because with her unfailing support, insights, and compassion, together we worked on my emotional health throughout the next several years. These wonderful, loving people, these angels, were put into my life to help me survive this unimaginable time and to help me thrive again.

As my birthday approached in March, I anticipated that the day would be emotionally draining for me. One thing that was especially important to me was to have a weekday Mass said for Dana. Besides that, I made no plans. I would simply let the day flow while being gentle with myself and staying in the present. My awareness was increasing every day as to what I needed to do to continue healing myself in an emotionally healthy way, and I persisted in that endeavor in every aspect of my life.

Journal entry: April 25, 2008 (recounting my birthday in March)

My birthday came and went without too much hoopla. Don't even remember much about what I did. We had a mass said for Dana. [I was trying to keep my sorrow under control during that Mass when] *I became acutely aware of what I now call God's revelation to me. When I was diagnosed with aggressive breast cancer in 1991 and my girls were 9 and 11 years old, I prayed to God, if it was His will, that I would live to at least see my daughters graduate from college. I knew that no matter when I die, it'll be difficult, but I so wanted to be there for Sarah and Dana to guide them and support them until they could be on their own. Anyway, this revelation came to me out of the blue. It's almost as if God tapped me on the shoulder* [and I heard Him whisper to me], *"Remember what you prayed for all those years ago, well I answered your prayer." It felt like a lightning bolt when I realized right then that He had given me the gift of my Dana for 25 years. That was my birthday gift this year—to be made aware again that life is precious and temporary and to be thankful to God that He loves me always and He answered my prayer—but in His way, not in my way!*

I could have been so very angry at God in that moment. But I had accepted the possibility of my God speaking to me if I only took the opportunity to listen. How had my heart been opened? From the first morning when we heard the news from the police, in my complete brokenness as a mother whose spirit was crushed and whose heart was broken into millions of pieces, I had placed myself in God's care. My God had carried me as He gently and lovingly guided me along my healing path.

I have reflected on all that has transpired from those first days, months, and even years as I have been writing this story. In doing so, I realized almost immediately there were so many signs of God taking care of me as I coped with our tragedy, as I began to heal, and as I began to define my new normal without Dana. First, I had come to the realization I was seeing the face of God in all who gathered to comfort and support us on that horrible Sunday afternoon when we returned home with Sarah. Then I had felt the unexpected, feathery, soothing touch on my shoulder that first night. And now I had my birthday revelation of the gift of Dana's life to me for twenty-five years.

I could have been too busy or too distracted to become aware of what I felt were signs or indications of God speaking to me, either through other people or to me directly. Or I could have simply chosen to ignore those signs and dismiss them as ridiculous imaginings. But I think I was open to God's tender, loving care because no one else could give me all I needed. What I have come to believe with every fiber of my being is that, if I try to keep an open heart and mind every day to listen and watch for God speaking to me, I am able to receive God's grace and His healing power. In our world and in our busy lives, that is a constant struggle for me. My goal each day is to find at least five to ten minutes of quiet time to spend with God. I admit I am not 100 percent successful with achieving that goal, but I can honestly say I miss those minutes of reflection and renewal when I do not take the time.

Dana's birthday is April 16, and I was fully cognizant this was next up on the days to get through in the first year after she died. There was no doubt in my mind that this day would be so much more difficult than my birthday. I did not actually dread the day as it approached, but I made a conscious decision ahead of time to leave my day open with no pressure to be committed to any schedule. In the end, I had taken care of myself the best way I knew how. Still, my Dana was forever physically gone, and my heart continued to be broken, seemingly never to be healed again.

Journal entry: April 25, 2008 (recounting Dana's birthday in April)

> *I took off of work and decided to leave the day open to do whatever I wanted to do in the moment. I started the day with a weekday mass celebrated for Dana. Linda [my sister-in-law] met me there. That mass was extremely hard for me emotionally, but since I find comfort and God's loving presence in church, I needed to get that sustenance.*
>
> *The day before I had called Katie [a girlfriend] to see if we could meet for coffee. Instead, she said to come over to her house. This April day was going to be magnificent. So, after mass, I drove there and we sat out on her deck overlooking Lake Michigan for 2 hours. We talked, we laughed, we cried, we looked at photos of Dana. I thank God for my close friends every day and Katie is an amazing woman and friend. With her, I never feel like I can't be 100% [sic] real and she is there just to be with me through whatever it is I'm feeling or sorting through.*
>
> *I went from there . . . to the mausoleum. I wanted to spend some time there that day. It was good to go and feel closer to Dana for a while. Then I went to a therapy session with Rita. What a blessing that session was because we talked mostly*

about Dana's birth and childhood into young adulthood and, in doing so, we truly celebrated her life. And talking with Rita was such an uplifting focus which helped me so much that day. I had watched the memorial video the night before—another positive but painful thing for me. It's all so bittersweet—I remembered and celebrated the gift of her life, but at the same time mourned what I'll never have again, in the physical sense.

On the way home from my therapy session, I just wanted to stop and be with Dana again for a few moments alone. Her girlfriends were there but they gave me some private time. Later I went over to the parents' of one of Dana's friends to visit with all of her girlfriends for a short time and to see Moose and just hug him. [Dana's dog lived with them now.]

Even though I made it through and did what I wanted to do, I was so exhausted for days afterward. I have found that to be the case any time I prepare for and survive any of these difficult days or events. Although I feel like I make it through, by the end of the day, I'm emotionally drained.

Slowly, slowly through these first several months of 2008, I had continued the process of defining my new normal. I fought that at times, because I did not want a new normal without Dana in our lives! But, little by little, I was becoming aware that even amidst the wrenching, aching loss of my child to murder, I did not want to be defined only by that. Surely, I must still have another role. My daughter's death did not make me less of a wife and a mother. I could never abandon my Sarah and had no intention of abandoning Joe, even as I continued to wonder if our marriage would survive this unimaginable tragedy. Surely Dana would want all of us to find happiness again.

Gradually, I had given myself permission to enjoy life whenever those moments presented themselves. Almost without me realizing it, those moments became more and more frequent as my survivor's guilt lessened and my emotional healing continued. Life has a funny way of moving on with or without us. We can let it pass us by or we can be an active participant. I was more consistently choosing to be an active participant again. The human spirit is exceptionally resilient, even when we do not want it to be.

CHAPTER 17

TANGLED WEB OF EMOTIONS

When we found out on August 19, 2007, that our daughter had been murdered the night before by a young man she had known and hung out with in college five to six years earlier, this nightmare seemed to me so much more horrifying than if it had been a stranger. All I could think was, *How was this possible? How could someone do this to another human being, much less a friend?* We knew little about Patrick Ford back then except that he had called 911, waited for them outside his apartment, and informed them he had tried to kill himself. I had never met him before, although Dana had talked about him a little bit all those years ago when they were in college together.

Once we began receiving the facts from the detective, my immediate reaction was one of instant skepticism and intense anger. Seriously? I could not accept, even for a second, that he had tried to kill himself. That was not a rational conclusion. I definitely was not rational, but in shock. I thought it might have been an excuse to make him look more sympathetic to us and to the police. Since I did not hear he had expressed sorrow for his actions, I concluded he did not care at all about what he had done to Dana, and I began to think of him as a "psycho monster." From that day forward, my perception of him did not change for several years. Other than that first reaction, during the entire week of preparation for the visitation, the funeral, and the burial, Patrick Ford was not on my mind at all. I was like a robot that had been programmed to just get each task done efficiently. My overriding goal was to have Dana's spirit present with us at the visitation and the funeral Mass.

Even amid my internal turmoil during those first several weeks after Dana's funeral and burial, I was struggling to make sense of what had happened and was simply trying to survive the searing pain and despair that overwhelmed me at times. At other times, I was sickened by the thought that Dana's murderer could have done such an evil deed. Yet through these conflicting emotions, I continued to focus on and question why this had happened to my Dana as I prayed for answers. Because the detectives had received no additional information from Patrick Ford about his motive, it appeared my prayers would remain unanswered. I concluded that he must have had some sort of mental break to do what he did. No one who is mentally and emotionally healthy would do something so horrific. Although that was my belief, it did not change my opinion that he did not care about what he had done to Dana. Yet when I reflect on that time, I do not believe I felt hatred toward him. However, I craved justice for Dana's murder. I wanted him to pay his debt to society for this inconceivable crime. At the time, I knew nothing at all about punishment options, only that I wanted him to be in jail for a long, long time. One thing I am certain of is that the death penalty never entered my thought process.

Dana's murderer was being held in Cook County Jail, one of the most horrible jails in the country. To be perfectly honest, I had been terrified he might be released from jail on bond while awaiting a trial. Since we had heard nothing from the investigative team as to any theories about motives, and we had absolutely no idea why he had killed Dana, I was so frightened that if he were released on bond, he could do the same thing to some other young woman or come after Sarah for some reason. What a huge relief it was, then, when we were informed he was not being released during the court proceedings.

During those first emotionally challenging weeks and months, I had overheard conversations among those who had no qualms about sharing what horrible things they hoped Dana's murderer was being subjected to while in Cook County Jail. Even then, I had cringed at the inhumanity of it all. Everyone has a right to his or her opinion, and I have no desire to be judge or jury here, but to me, their words were disturbing. When I could do so, I removed myself from those conversations that I felt were poisonous to my already broken spirit. I learned something invaluable about myself from those experiences; I became aware of the fact that I could not live a life filled with hatred and revenge. Living like that would destroy my heart, my soul, and my spirit. I never had any desire for horrible things to happen to him in jail. My instincts told me being incarcerated would be punishment enough. And in the short term, Cook County Jail would be a fitting place for him as far as I was concerned.

As the months passed, I persisted in the work of healing my broken heart and spirit. This was an incredibly slow process. Something deep inside of me, most likely my spirit and my desire to live again, kept me moving forward no matter how many times I was tempted to give in to my despair and heartbreak. I chose to move away from the darkness and agony over losing my Dana and instead move toward the light, toward seeing her life as a gift from God. And I chose to do whatever I needed to do to keep from destroying my spirit and my soul. These choices I made along the way finally led me to see a dim light in the distance. Once I became aware of that faraway light, it became my beacon. It inspired me to keep moving forward with the hope and faith I could find happiness, joy, and peace again.

Almost from the beginning of this horrible nightmare, I had never doubted Dana most likely would have forgiven her murderer. Sometime in early 2008, within six months of Dana's murder, I became conscious of a nagging voice in my head that occasionally surfaced uninvited. At first when I noticed it, I put it out of my mind. But this little voice or whisper was persistent. I did not want to even acknowledge the voice within or reflect on it, so when I heard it I fought hard to push it out of my mind. But that did not seem to be working. What was I hearing that had me in such a quandary?

Could I ever truly forgive this "psycho monster"? Not condone his actions or ever forget what he did, but forgive him?

I knew this was one of those roadblocks I did have some control over. However, at this point in my tenuous healing journey, it was inconceivable that I could ever get to a place where I could forgive Patrick Ford. It seemed utterly impossible. I knew in my heart, of course, that this is what our God asks of us. But honestly, I did not want to forgive him. And I was annoyed that I continued to hear that little voice off and on. Why wouldn't it just go away?

I had been taught the power of God's message is that when we forgive others, our God will forgive us. In those moments when I have let go of grudges or forgiven someone for hurting me, my spirit has been set free and I have felt so much lighter. But how could God ask me to forgive someone who had murdered my Dana? I wanted no part of that in those early months of 2008.

Surely, God, there must be exceptions. I know You taught us we are called to love our enemies and to pray for those who hurt us. If we only love those who love us, how difficult is that? But You cannot be serious in wanting me to forgive this young man who murdered Dana!

This became my ongoing struggle during the next few years. It was not something I obsessed about or even thought about regularly. But whenever that little voice whispered to me, I reflected on where I was in my healing journey. At times, I cried because of this huge weight I felt. And eventually I prayed for God to help me forgive, even though I didn't know how He could ever accomplish that in me.

CHAPTER 18

NEVER IN MY WILDEST DREAMS

In early February of 2008, I had driven down to the Criminal Court Building to talk once again with our prosecutor as well as with our victim specialist. Each time I met with them, I got a better picture of what had transpired that horrible night. Even so, it became quite apparent that we would never get the whole story of what had driven this individual to murder Dana. But what did become crystal clear to me was that I would eventually participate in the court proceedings and would attend the trial, if there were a trial, sometime in the future.

Journal entry: March 4, 2008 (recounting meeting with prosecutor)

I know now that I will attend the trial. I am and always will be Dana's mom. I tried to protect her, as moms do, from getting hurt so many times. But, as we all know, we can't always do that. So, as she grew into adulthood, I would at least try to walk with her and support her as best as I could in her trials and tribulations. I couldn't protect her that night or be with her when she died, but I can be with her and walk that road with her by being at the trial. As painful as it will be, I feel like I know almost everything that the prosecutor can share with me. And I've survived hearing all of that—God has taken care of my emotional health through it all. And I'm leaving it in God's hands to take care of me through the trial.

My participation in the court proceedings began in April 2008. Status hearings had been held approximately every month since

September 2007. I had not yet been ready to show up at one, and I cannot honestly remember why I chose this day. But I knew I was as ready as I was ever going to be to face the accused murderer and participate in the status hearings of the case. My sister Cindy had driven down from Wisconsin to be with me. Sarah met us at the courthouse, and Joe decided to come from work to meet us there. I was extremely grateful to have the support of my family. And as I had done in the past, I put my faith in God to take care of the emotional health of me and my family this day.

I had had a glimpse of the workings down at the Criminal Court Building when I had been chosen as a juror on a criminal case a few years earlier. To me, it is a scary place down on the South Side of Chicago in a rough, crime-ridden neighborhood. When Sarah and I had our first meeting with our prosecutor right before Thanksgiving 2007, we had met Mike at his office in that building and had gotten a taste of the security process and the general atmosphere. This is the courthouse for many of the criminal cases in Cook County. The halls and courtrooms were filled with individuals out on bail who were there to attend their status hearings, as well as lawyers, judges, policemen and women, jurors, and visitors. It was easy for me to feel intimidated.

Never in my wildest dreams had I imagined I would be in the middle of this scenario, being the mother of a murdered daughter attending the status hearing of her accused murderer. That just did not have a place in my world—it did not compute. It happened to others, but not to me. Nevertheless, here I was, soon to see Patrick Ford for the first time and feeling sick to my stomach. How would I react to seeing this young man, the accused murderer of my daughter, when he entered the courtroom?

Our small group entered the courtroom and found space to sit together on a bench. Our victim specialist, Pam, joined us as we waited for our case to be called by the judge. We learned that there were strict courtroom rules we were expected to observe: no talking on cell phones or taking pictures, no newspapers, no talking loudly or disrupting the proceedings, no outbursts, no sleeping on the benches! Since my stomach was already quite nauseated, it was good there were so many distractions all around us, from the various visitors coming in and out of the gallery where we sat to lawyers, courtroom personnel, and police officers doing the same. All of that kept me from dwelling too much on why I was there and what my reaction would be once I saw Patrick Ford for the first time.

Our wait seemed interminable, and then, after what felt like an eternity, the judge announced a recess, stood up, and left the courtroom with no further words. At that point Joe rose, disgusted with the whole experience, and announced he was driving back to work. Since the rest of us had no idea how long the recess would be, we stayed in the courtroom because we did not want to miss the judge when he returned and called our case. I felt like I was living in a criminal-court TV drama. But there were differences too. There was a glass wall separating us in the gallery from the judge, the defendant, and the attorneys. There were a few flyers taped to the glass wall, which made it difficult to get a clear view. In addition, it was difficult for us to hear when the judge, lawyers, or a defendant spoke. I found that all quite annoying, as if I could do anything about it!

When the judge had returned and our case was finally called, I steeled myself for the moment when Patrick Ford would be brought into the courtroom. I was very nervous because I did not want to break down in the gallery and I had no idea how I would react. When the deputy finally escorted the accused into the courtroom, they were facing us for a few brief moments before Patrick Ford was instructed to turn and face the judge. In those few seconds, I saw the face of the accused murderer before he put his head down and turned to face the judge with his hands behind his back. Shockingly, seeing him in the flesh for the first time, I did not break down. And what surprised me most was my first impression of him.

He looked like any of the typical, well-groomed young men I knew, friends of my daughters, sons of my friends, and my own nephews. What had I expected? Other than being in a prisoner jumpsuit, he was clean shaven, had short hair, no visible tattoos, and he was subdued as he faced the judge with his hands crossed behind his back. He appeared to be respectful of the judge and he stood completely still. Since I had thought of this young man as a "psycho monster," it was not the impression I had built up in my head. Because I had thought he was psychotic or had had a mental breakdown, I guess I had expected to see a prisoner who would, at first sight, have intimidated me, one who seemed menacing or threatening, one who may have been disheveled in his appearance and who might have been combative or arrogant in responding to the judge's questions. This expectation clearly and sadly was based on my judging him without knowing anything about him.

Not much happened at the status hearing that was of significance to us. I did not learn anything new, and Patrick Ford did not speak. I should have realized right then this was going to be an excruciating, drawn-out process. Nevertheless, I was firm in my decision to be involved for the long haul, no matter what happened. I believe that, subconsciously, back then I did not know if I would be able to fully move on after Dana's murder until we got justice. I continued to attend the court status hearings regarding Patrick Ford's case from that point on, first with my sister-in-law Linda, and then on my own after several months.

CHAPTER 19

FIRST ANNIVERSARY OF DANA'S DEATH

They whom we love and lost are no longer where they were before.
They are now wherever we are.
—Saint John Chrysostom

Without a doubt, the first anniversary of Dana's death took the biggest toll on my body, mind, and spirit. I do not have a clear memory of when I decided to have a service of some kind on the anniversary of her death. What I do know is I had an intense, burning desire to celebrate my daughter's life in some positive way instead of simply focusing on the brutality of her death. I had no idea what constituted a memorial service. I wanted it to be a prayer service as well as a celebration of her young life, if possible.

In early summer, I discussed my desire to have a service on August 18 with Joe and Sarah. I sensed they both realized how much it would mean to me and agreed to be there with me that day, under one condition. They asked that I keep the number of guests small so as not to be overwhelming. In respect to their wishes, I agreed to limit the people I would have invited to a select few. Joe just wanted his small family with us, Sarah wanted only a few close friends, and I invited a few of Dana's closest friends as well as several of my dearest friends who had traveled with me and had been there unconditionally for me during the past year.

Once that decision was made, I realized I needed some guidance from Father Jim, our friend and the priest who had officiated at

Dana's funeral Mass. I hoped he would agree to officiate at this service, and I would simply help him wherever he needed me. Since I wanted to incorporate both religious and nonreligious segments, I questioned whether that would be possible. We corresponded a few times and he agreed to participate in the service. Father Jim would be going on vacation for a few weeks, so he asked me to think about what I wanted while he was gone. As I reflected on that, I got a bit panicked. How was I supposed to do this by myself? By the time he returned, there would only be a few weeks before the service!

I realized I could get nothing accomplished, or I could put on paper the service I had formulated in my head and be ready to review it with him upon his return. Thinking through those two options made my decision easy. So, as I designed the program for this special occasion, the only segments I was sure I wanted to include would be a eulogy about my daughter's amazing legacy and Sarah's eulogy to her sister. There was much we each wanted to share about the most precious gift of Dana in our lives and her love for us, especially since we had not been able to do so at her funeral Mass. The rest of the program fell into place as I poured all my energy, my heart, and my soul into designing this first memorial service for Dana, a service which Father Jim and I would celebrate together.

After Father Jim and I reviewed the entire program and the order of the service, he was fine with it, and we were good to go! A sense of relief flooded me and a feeling of peace came over me as I felt that I had done all I could. I smiled to myself as the thought crossed my mind that this may have been God's plan all along, nudging me to design the service. I realized as soon as I had completed the program for the memorial service, which would be a celebration of Dana's short life with us, the entire process had already been healing for me.

Once the program was set, my next decision was where to have our memorial service. The Immaculate Heart of Mary Garden Mausoleum at All Saints Cemetery, that beautiful space surrounded by the splendor of nature, was exactly where I wanted to celebrate Dana's life on the day of our memorial service. To this day, whenever I visit the cemetery and the mausoleum setting, a sense of peace, calmness, and serenity envelops me. I can feel God's loving presence in this sacred space for all who have gone before us. This was the perfect choice for our first memorial service.

Journal entry: August 15, 2008

> It's been one week since Dana had come home last year at this time for a two week visit. Last Friday, I was sitting on my front patio on a beautiful afternoon when the memories came flooding back. I relived the moment she pulled into the driveway that Friday late afternoon. I happened to be across the street talking to my neighbors . . . Right then she turned into our street, parked in the driveway, and she and Moosie came over . . . She let us know what a LONG drive it had been from Minneapolis, but gave me a hug. Then she was her warm, friendly self as we all talked for a few minutes . . . And it's one of my most strong memories of her from that week we had with her before she died.
>
> I cherish it. But that reliving of last year started my incredible grief that day. I later read a letter that arrived that afternoon from one of my sisters, Cindy, who said she admired me so much for my courage and ability to talk about Daney. She said when our mom died, she doesn't remember anyone talking about her at all, so it was another huge loss to her. It wasn't until she was an adult that she could talk about mom without crying. Everything in that letter struck a nerve and allowed all of my sadness, loneliness, and feelings of loss to surface . . . When I read her words, the floodgates opened. As I talked to her later that day, we shared our sadness about us as children losing our mom and losing any chance to keep her memory alive, because of our dysfunctional family.
>
> I don't think of myself as courageous at all right now. I just know, that for me to survive this indescribable tragedy,

I have to be able to talk about Dana, and be able to keep her memory alive for myself and for those who come after us that are her family . . . I knew I would start calling those close girlfriends to try to spend some time with them. They nourish my soul. They let me be me, good or bad, happy or sad. They are all mothers & in their guts can relate at a deep level with how this is affecting me. They are my lifeline when I feel like I'm drowning. They are God's gifts to me.

This past week I've had waves of sadness as I remember things Dana & I did together that week last year . . . I have been planning a memorial service that will take place on Monday, August 18. I have put my heart and soul into this and know it will be very special and healing for me. I hope it will be that way for all who we've invited. It's just Joe's family, and a few of Sarah's close friends, a few of Dana's friends, and several of my friends . . . The people I've invited are those who have traveled with me this past year and have been there for me unconditionally. It will be a prayer service, as well as a memorial service to celebrate Dana's short but meaningful life. I pray that God will continue to comfort and embrace me as I struggle through the next several days of ups and downs.

As we all met at the mausoleum on August 18, 2008, it was a most beautiful, sunny day. From the start of this day, the glorious weather lightened my mood significantly. Sarah and I had arrived early with a few of my girlfriends to get the music set up, the flowers arranged, balloons anchored for a launch later, and the programs ready to hand out. I knew I would also need that time to get myself quieted and settled before everybody else arrived. Up until this point, all day I was living on the edge of remaining in the present or plunging into the depths of despair. I prayed I would keep it together for our service and for my daughter.

Once everyone was there with us, our memorial service began with an opening hymn by Liam Lawton called "In the Quiet." I had first heard that song at Dana's funeral Mass. As I had listened to the lyrics that horrible day, the words had pierced my already shattered heart, yet at the same time touched me to the core of my being as if I were being held in the loving and tender embrace of my God in all my brokenness. This hauntingly beautiful song became one of the songs I listened to nightly as I tried to sleep and as I prayed, always in the quiet.

I chose that song to set the tone for my theme of reflecting on our healing journeys during this first painful year. We continued with an opening prayer by Father Jim, a Bible reading by a friend of Sarah's, and a time for Father Jim to say a few words of reflection. One of Dana's closest friends and a dear friend of mine then read our prayers of petition, after which Father Jim concluded these prayers of the faithful. A time of meditation followed as we listened to another beautiful song. Next, Sarah and I read our eulogies, after which we allowed some time for anyone who wished to do so to share a memory or story about Dana. Father Jim then led us all in praying the "Our Father" and concluded the service with a final blessing. In celebration of Dana's life, we finished the memorial service by sending up balloons toward heaven with our love while listening to the song "I Will Remember You," sung by Sarah McLachlan. As we all released our balloons into the sky, they headed southeast toward Wrigley Field. Since Dana was such a diehard Cubs fan, the significance was not lost on us. We enjoyed a chuckle about Dana letting us know she was there with us.

This beautiful celebration of Dana's life was exactly what I had needed that day. As heart wrenching as it had been to speak my thoughts out loud and listen to Sarah's pain and sorrow as she read her tribute, I believe it was healing for us both to share our thoughts and memories of our Dana. In addition, I had given all invitees notice there would be a time for anyone who wished to do so to share a story or a memory of their relationship with Dana. The weight of my loss had been lightened just a bit as I had listened to and laughed at the stories shared by friends and family. The entire service from beginning to end truly had helped me file away the horrific memories of the events last year and, instead, plant these beautiful memories close to my heart. My hope was that it had also helped those loved ones who had shared the service with us. Afterward we had invited those guests who could join us to share a meal, continue our celebration, and enjoy our friendship.

Even though the day was all I had hoped for and more, it was not without its distressing moments. I had become aware at some point during the service that neither Joe nor Sarah had chosen to come stand with me. Instead, Joe had planted himself along the opposite wall between his two sisters, appearing to be holding up that wall as if his life depended on it. Sarah had been near but with her boyfriend. At one point, in a moment of clarity, I had felt so alone standing there without Sarah or Joe at my side. But sadly and regrettably, I had never asked them to come stand up front with me. I think I was so overwhelmed with sadness that my way of holding myself together had been to focus 100 percent on directing this memorial service exactly as I had designed it. For several days, I berated myself for having been so preoccupied that I did not ask Sarah and Joe to join me. Eventually, though, I took my own advice to be gentle on myself and came to accept that we had each survived the day the best we could manage.

Journal entry: August 31, 2008 (recounting the memorial service)

The prayer/memorial service was all I hoped for and more. I experienced it to be intimate, personal, spiritual, comforting, healing, and reflective. We prayed for Dana, for all of us there to help us in our healing journey, and for all who could not be with us but are struggling with our loss of an amazing young woman in our lives. We cried, we laughed, and we listened to memories, thoughts, feelings, and stories from family and friends. We heard beautiful songs, we celebrated Dana and how she left a remarkable legacy. We celebrated and reflected that, hopefully, we all have been changed for the better because of what we each learned from Dana and her presence in our lives.

A year has passed since my beautiful daughter's life was taken. Sometimes it just seems like she's still in Minnesota at Vet School and hasn't come home yet. I'm not in denial, but it's weird how it can just seem that way at times. At other times, in my darkest moments, when I feel like my heart is breaking, I am brought back to reality in the most painful sense. In those moments, I grieve and cry for what is lost to me and what I'll never have again. In my eulogy [at the memorial service], *I quoted Kahlil Gibran. His beautiful words, "When you are sorrowful, look again in your heart, and you shall see that in truth you are weeping for that which has been your delight," have brought me comfort as I am healing this past year. When I was composing the eulogy and crying as I wrote all of the things I miss about Dana and my relationship with her, the significance of Gibran's words reminded me that all of those sad memories ARE the same ones that fill me with comfort and peace. Those same memories are "that which has been my delight" and I will always have them in my heart as long as I live. NO ONE, not even Dana's murderer, can take that away from me!*

Since Dana died, my own personal journey of loss, suffering, and healing has brought me to where I am at this moment. I am at a more peaceful place. I will always have times of sadness and a pain in my heart that Dana is not here with us through milestones and even in the most mundane of situations. But, I am learning to live fully and celebrate each day, each moment of my time left on this earth. I have been given the gift of life, still, and I want to cherish what I have, who I am, and what God continues to bless me with.

I have learned that, more than ever before, I must take care of my spirit. I have found so many ways to do that and

I need to practice these things EVERY day. It is what has gotten me through this first year and what will continue to help me heal. There is still so much to deal with as the trial looms in the future: the incredibly frustrating slowness of the process, the fear of him (Patrick Ford) somehow getting off or even getting a lesser verdict than first degree murder, the anxiety of how I'll make it through [a trial] and be able to sit through it all (because I really want to and need to), and the ever-present realization that we'll never find out what exactly happened.

With all that said, I have become so much better at letting things go that are out of my control. Everything I listed above is out of my control, except how I will get through the trial. So, for the most part, I've let the rest go most of the time. I can't and won't live my life obsessing over that stuff.

As far as my attending the trial, I will use those tools I've been using all year. And God has gotten me through this year, every step of the way. Every time I've prepared to hear horrible things about the case and Dana's murder, I felt God's loving presence and, even though it was heartbreaking to hear it, I felt better knowing the truth. Every time I've prepared to get through another "anniversary" moment—first Thanksgiving, Christmas, Dana's birthday, Mother's Day, day of Dana's death—I survive and learn more about myself through the experience if I only open myself up and let myself feel all of the various feelings. I have learned to take care of myself.

CHAPTER 20

A BETTER PLACE

Christmas is a magic time for some and a difficult one for others. As another Christmas approached, Joe, Sarah, and I were still not ready to host our annual festivities. Instead, Joe and I drove into Chicago to share a delicious dinner hosted by Sarah and her boyfriend, after which we drove back to the suburbs. There Sarah, Joe, and I attended Christmas Eve Mass at St. James Church. Unlike last Christmas, when I could not bear to attend St. James, this evening I longed to celebrate the birth of the Christ child with our community. I allowed myself to be immersed in the Mass as the beautiful traditions, the rituals, the narrative of Jesus's birth, and the church music of the Christmas season replenished my spirit and grounded me.

Even though at times my intense sadness brought tears to my eyes, here in this sacred space I found the solace, comfort, and peace I so yearned for this night. Amidst the darkness there was also light and so much to be thankful for. I had been blessed with a loving and sensitive daughter, Sarah, who was my rock at church that night. Whenever I began to break down and cry, she was there to comfort me, to hug me or hold my hand. Our little family was there together at this joy-filled Christmas Eve Mass in spite of our loss and brokenness, and I believed Dana was right there with us. My healing journey had brought me to this moment this night, filled with wonder and thanksgiving for all I continued to be blessed with, filled with hope for our continued growth and healing. I could not think of a better place to be at this moment, feeling that my God would always be with me in my sorrows and in my joy.

Our Christmas Day was supposed to be relaxing with no schedule to follow. We would simply be in the present and let the day flow. All of us looked forward to being together, taking it easy, opening our gifts to each other, and enjoying our traditional lasagna dinner. Instead, we had an unusual day. The following was my last official journal entry and summarizes my emotional state, my amazing progress, and where I chose to go from there next as 2008 came to a close.

Journal entry: December 25, 2008

It is Christmas day. Nothing this past week has gone smoothly according to my plans! I am sitting at the Veterinary Specialty Clinic with Riley. He has not been himself and was totally lethargic this morning. So I've been here for at least three hours. It's given me time to reflect and do some of my life renewing activities this morning. It's reminded me of those things I know I need to continue to do for myself— things that will refresh my spirit and give my heart some peace.

[*The Death of a Child: Reflections for Grieving Parents*, written by Elaine Stillwell, is a book that had such a profound impact on helping me to begin to heal in the early days after Dana died. In my journaling here, I paraphrase several of the activities the author shares that closely matched what I had been practicing in my healing journey.]

These life renewing activities give me solace and also can rescue me on a bad day:
1. Have coffee/breakfast/lunch/dinner with a friend(s)
2. Spend some time with nature, i.e. Botanic Gardens, walk along the lake, Millennium Park in Chicago, etc.
3. Listen to soothing music
4. Prayer

5. *Letting myself cry/mourn*
6. *Quiet time to meditate/reflect/remember*
7. *Taking a walk on a beautiful day*
8. *Reading grief resources*
9. *Journaling*
10. *Continue to keep Dana's memory alive; be the keeper of the memories and work with organizations we donate to in her memory: PAWS (Pets Are Worth Saving), Anti-Cruelty Society, Susan G. Komen For The Cure, University of Minnesota Scholarship and Endowment Fund*
11. *Keep in touch with Dana's close friends. I feel close to her through them.*
12. *Focus on looking at life in a positive frame of mind; count my blessings of what I still have, what has graced my life, and what resources are available to help journey through grief*
13. *Encircle myself with compassionate listeners, those friends and family who will let me be me. They let me feel my loss and not minimize it, ignore it, or try to fix it. They let me cry, talk about Dana, look at pictures with me, share stories. They encircle me with their love and caring ways. I know they'll let me grieve for as long as and loud as I need without judging.*

Of course, today is a difficult day. I am just trying to feel the feelings and remember and concentrate on the sweet memories. But, equally as important, I want to fully experience and enjoy this day with Joe and Sarah. I am committed to living my life fully and being present to those who are still a part of my life, who I love and who love me. Dana will be there with us.

I have come so far in the last several months. I can finally say I have been able to let go of the anger I have felt toward Joe in his way of handling his grief journey. I cannot control what he can or cannot do as far as sharing with me. I can still be sad that we are not able to share our grief. But I can find others who are able to let me express myself—those compassionate listeners. It is part of my journey to let go of things I have no control over and just deal with what I can control. I am more at peace about that now.

As 2008 ended, I was in awe at the realization that sometime during the previous few months, I had no longer felt that undeniable resentment toward Joe because he could not be there for me. I had been healing for a little over a year by that time. My rational self was finally able to accept that which I already knew, but my emotional self had not been able to accept until then; everyone needs to grieve in their own unique way. I had let go of my need and wish for Joe to share his grief with me, and I had finally accepted him for where he was in his healing journey. I had come to terms with the fact that I had no control over how Joe was handling his grief. I could not explain how this change of heart had come about, but I was convinced God had been at work in me, helping me to heal! I felt so much lighter without all that anger weighing me down. What an incredible gift of grace I was given as I acknowledged that nothing is impossible with God.

But don't get me wrong, sometimes I was still unhappy and aggravated that we could not share in this loss. Why would I stay in my marriage when I knew my husband could not find a way to share himself emotionally with me? I still had much work to do on myself because Dana had been murdered just a little over a year before. I do not believe I had the strength or the will to make any long-term decisions about my marriage. My hope remained that someday Joe and I would share our memories of our life with Dana, laughing together, crying together, and healing together. With the future still so uncertain because of the ongoing court process, my emotional healing journey steadily continued as I solely focused on my own healing. And thankfully, I knew I had been blessed with my sisterhood of women friends and my daughter, who would continue to walk this journey with me.

CHAPTER 21

THE EXCRUCIATINGLY SLOW COURT PROCESS

As we turned the calendar to another new year, Joe, Sarah, and I had all settled into our own routines. Life does move on, and in 2009, all three of us continued along our healing paths, each in our own unique way. As for me, I continued to appear at any status hearing regarding Patrick Ford's case. Little did I know back when I started attending these hearings in April 2008 how clueless I was about the entire legal process that occurred before a trial date was even scheduled. Even though I had served as a member of a jury panel on a criminal case several years earlier, I was in for a rude awakening as to what must happen before a trial even began!

Desperately craving justice for my daughter's murder, I was anxious to have a speedy process. I wanted a guilty verdict so Dana's murderer could pay his debt to society for his crime. But so badly desiring that quick outcome could not make it happen. Instead, the interminable snail's pace of progress in getting justice was maddening at times and certainly frustrating as the weeks, months, and years passed!

Patrick Ford, the defendant, had initially entered a formal plea of not guilty to the charges against him. That plea had then set in motion the legal criminal proceedings against him. If a defendant's plea is not guilty, it may take several months (or more) for the case to progress to the point where the judge sets a date for trial. There are many court hearings in the intervening months, approximately one per month. At any point the judge may make rulings that determine how, and if, the case will proceed.

During the time before the trial, the prosecution and the defense complete their pretrial discovery of facts and conduct their own independent investigations of the evidence as they consider trial strategy. This pretrial discovery phase involves the exchange of documents and lists of witnesses between the prosecutor and defense attorney. The defendant may change a plea at any time during the process and avoid a trial.

In our criminal justice system, a defendant is presumed innocent until proven guilty. To obtain a conviction, the prosecution must prove the defendant is guilty beyond a reasonable doubt. I was greatly reassured as I saw how fastidious and conscientious our prosecution team was in their investigation and in following the strict letter of the law. Intellectually, I appreciated that they must proceed carefully, dotting all the i's and crossing all the t's, to best ensure they would get a conviction that could not be overturned later. Even so, the slow progress and my vulnerability while still grieving made the entire process painful for me at times and emotionally and physically draining. Yet I was committed to going to the court hearings regularly. That resolve never diminished.

Without a doubt, as I had become more aware of what was going on around me each month when I was at the Cook County Criminal Court Building and in the courtroom, my whole perspective changed. The effects of a murder know no boundaries. I was now one of those parents experiencing the depth of despair and loss that the families of murdered loved ones experienced every single day in the Chicagoland area. Thank God for Pam, our victim specialist, who sat with me in the courtroom each month. I could count on either Pam or a substitute to always be there for me to explain what was going on and to support me in whatever way I needed.

After the first hearing Joe, Sarah, and I had attended, my sister-in-law Linda traveled down to the Cook County Criminal Court Building with me for the next several months. I am eternally grateful for the love, courage, and support she so freely gave me during those months. Eventually, though, she could no longer take off work on a weekday to accompany me to court. From then on, I drove down on my own, confident that Pam, or a substitute if she was delayed for some reason, would show up to sit there with me. That knowledge comforted me.

There were few status hearings that did not leave me either frustrated or angry. And that was not any one individual's fault, but most often was due to the tedious criminal court process. In the beginning, my perception of how justice worked and how evidence was gathered and processed relatively quickly came from watching too many TV shows! I was gently reminded early on that this was not reality TV. But oh, how I wished it were back then. During our discovery phase, there was an incredible amount of evidence to be obtained and shared with the defense team, such as documents, medical records, police reports, and physical objects. From my perspective, no one piece of evidence seemed to be easily obtained. I certainly learned much as the months and years went on about why court cases can take years to get a resolution.

There were often motions that were ruled on during a status hearing. A motion is an oral or written request by the prosecution or defense asking the judge to consider and rule on a legal matter. Sometimes the motion was accepted, sometimes it was denied. But arguably the most frustrating for me were the motions extended to the next status hearing. That was just delaying the process once again.

There were several court delays in which I showed up for a status hearing and waited in the courtroom for our case to be called, only to find out there would not be a status hearing that day. This occurred for varying reasons: there had been a mix-up and the defendant was not brought to court; the defense attorney was delayed and the judge could not wait any longer so rescheduled the hearing for the following month; the judge had to take a recess and the defense attorney could not wait for him to return; the judge was ill and the substitute judge simply rescheduled for the following month. These instances heightened my level of frustration with the court system as another example of our justice being delayed! And there were so many other delays.

For our prosecutor to obtain the defendant's medical records from the hospital where the police had taken him on August 19, 2007, Mike had to request for the judge to obtain them. The hospital would not release them without a court order because of the patient privacy laws (HIPAA). As of February 2008, those medical records still had not been released. But eventually the prosecution team did get access to them.

A search warrant had been issued early in the process to take possession of the defendant's computer, which the prosecution obtained in a timely manner. However, once that had been accomplished, they were stymied in being able to access any actual information. Our prosecutor then filed a motion requesting that the judge allow a search for any information stored on the computer that would be pertinent to the case. That caused another delay! Finally, toward the end of 2008, the prosecution was granted approval. After all this time, there was nothing of evidentiary value!

We were informed that the crucial crime lab evidence obtained in the criminal investigation, such as DNA samples, fingerprints, etc., had been sent to the crime lab as priority items. As a result, the prosecution would most likely have the results within six months. The results trickled in beginning in February 2008. But the last of the crime lab results were not turned over to the defense attorney until late in 2008, about a full year after those samples had been obtained!

One of the biggest mysteries involved cell phones. Dana's cell phone and two others had been recovered at the crime scene. The investigative team accessed the information from Dana's phone. A second cell phone was identified as that of the defendant, but information on that phone was not actually obtained until the end of 2008. And what was discovered after all those months was that he had not used that phone since May 2007! Back to the drawing board. The third phone recovered at the crime scene, which the police thought had been Dana's phone, was locked. As far as I knew, Dana never had a second cell phone or an account with that cellular phone company, all of which I had shared with the police early on. In their defense, they could not take the word of a mother of a twenty-five-year-old as a guarantee. The police technician, working on that third phone, finally confirmed in late 2008 that this phone had also been identified as Patrick Ford's phone! For some reason, though, over a year after the crime, this third phone was still locked. The judge in our case was not happy because this frustrating situation was holding up the completion of the pretrial discovery phase. The criminal court case could not move forward until this stage was completed. Since the judge knew the locked phone belonged to the defendant, a new police technician was given the tasks of getting that phone unlocked and pulling any information from it!

This second police technician, also unable to unlock it, brought the phone to the cell phone company for their help in doing so. However, the phone company stated that unlocking the phone would reset everything to the factory settings, thereby deleting any important clues that might be contained within. At the beginning of 2009, the phone was then shipped to FBI technicians in Washington, DC, who were given the task of unlocking the phone. Our prosecution team wanted to leave no stone unturned, so if there happened to be any evidence helpful to our case, they wanted that information! Finally, in May 2009, the FBI unlocked the phone. Our prosecutor, Mike, turned all the data over to the defense team, but after all that time, they found no useful information.

Now, almost two years after this phase had begun, all we were waiting for were the mental health evaluations from both the defense and the prosecution teams. How much longer must we wait to get resolution? I had been warned that conducting the defendant's evaluations would be a slow process. Therefore, I was not hopeful the discovery phase would be completed soon.

For me, it never went unnoticed that the defendant usually entered the courtroom with his head down and stood motionless before the judge. Honestly, other than noticing, I did not think much more about his presence. I realized that, when asked by a few close friends how I could deal with seeing him each time, this must have been my way of protecting myself from whatever feelings might have surfaced had I focused on him. Instead I kept myself 100 percent focused on the proceedings. That is how I could continue to attend every month.

Sarah (left), four years old, and Dana, eighteen months old

Sarah (left), Dana, and Joe at a Chicago Cubs' spring-training baseball game in Phoenix, Arizona, on March 27, 2005

Dana (left) and Barb at Sarah's twenty-seventh
birthday-party barbeque with family on September 4, 2006

Sarah (left) and Dana at
Blue Agave in Chicago on September 8, 2006

Our 2006 Christmas-card photo taken on Thanksgiving (11/23/06); from left to right: Sarah, Barb with Riley, Joe, and Dana with Moose

Sarah (left), Joe, and Dana on our family vacation in Naples, Florida, in March 2007

Sarah (left) and Dana having fun at Howl at the Moon, a piano bar in Chicago, on May 18, 2007

From left to right: Sarah, Dana, Barb, and Joe at Dana's graduation from Midwestern University with a master's in biomedical science on May 26, 2007

Dana and her dog, Moose, posing in our backyard in the summer of 2007, not long before she moved to Minneapolis, Minnesota

Barb (left) and Sarah hiking in Rocky Mountain National Park on November 10, 2007, while visiting family in Estes Park, Colorado

Barb (left) and Sarah at her graduation from
University of Chicago with a master's in business
administration on December 8, 2007

Barb (left), Sarah with Riley, and Joe at
our house before leaving to go to our first
memorial service for Dana on August 18, 2008

From left to right: Joe, Sarah, and Barb posing on a bridge over Sol Duc Falls on the Olympic Peninsula in Washington state on September 5, 2008

Joe (left) and Barb celebrating with Sarah on her birthday on September 4, 2011, while vacationing in Hilton Head, South Carolina

CHAPTER 22

TRIAL OR NO TRIAL?

At what point in the discovery phase had it been decided to have mental health evaluations completed for the defendant? Going back to the spring of 2008, Patrick Ford's defense attorney asked our prosecutor if we would make a plea agreement offer. Joe and I had no idea what to think of this request or what that all entailed. Why would we want to make this kind of offer? So in early May 2008, we met with our prosecutor, Mike, to become educated about this request, to decide if we even wanted to make an offer, and if so, what our offer might be.

Mike patiently answered all our questions and concerns that day. In some cases, the prosecutor and the defense attorney will negotiate the disposal of a case without a trial. The prosecutor will ask for a specific punishment in exchange for the defendant's guilty plea. This is called a plea agreement. If we made an offer for Patrick Ford to plead guilty to first-degree murder and he accepted our terms, there would be no trial, no chance of parole, nor of any appeals later. And if there were no trial, then there would be no risk of the defendant getting a lesser charge with a much shorter prison sentence, nor of the defendant being found not guilty and being released from prison! Our decision was easy. We wanted to make an offer.

Mike discussed with us what would be a fair and just offer based on the crime. That was important because if the offer were accepted by the defense and the defendant, the judge in the case would also have to approve the first-degree murder charge, as well as the sentence stated in the offer. If the judge did not agree the sentence was fair and just, based on all aspects of the crime, the prosecution would have to revise the offer. With Mike's guidance and his knowledge of the law, all three of us finally agreed that a forty-year prison sentence with the charge of first-degree murder would be appropriate, which Mike felt the judge would accept. If they accepted our offer, Patrick Ford would serve the entire sentence minus time already served in Cook County Jail. No parole hearings or appeals would be allowed. We left Mike that afternoon with the knowledge he would present the offer to the defense attorney at the first opportunity.

Our prosecutor had presented our offer to the defense attorney sometime before the next status hearing in June 2008. Through this entire criminal court process, Mike and I had convened periodically after a status hearing so he could explain anything I did not understand. It was in one of those meetings after the June 2008 status hearing that Mike shared with me what the defense attorney's decision had been to our offer. Patrick Ford's attorney had had little reaction to the news. He was not shocked, he took no offense to the offer, but he quickly and simply stated that the defense team would have to get the defendant evaluated for insanity before they would even consider it!

Even as I write about that development now, over nine years later, I feel that anger and frustration building up. My first thought had been, *Why did his attorney even ask us to come up with an offer if he knew the defense team would refuse it?* And then, *Was he trying to see how short of a sentence we would offer, hoping we wanted to avoid a trial so badly that we would give them an offer they could not refuse?*

As I ranted about that in our prosecutor's office that day, Mike convinced me not to read too much into it because we would never get an explanation. The defense attorney was certainly not going to share his strategy with us! So, the pretrial discovery phase continued on, with the defense attorney eventually hiring a psychiatrist to evaluate the defendant's mental health. Once that doctor was finished with the evaluation, our prosecutor would most likely request a psychiatrist to do an evaluation.

Reawakening

In September 2009, I learned from our prosecutor that he had finally obtained the mental health evaluations from the defense team's psychiatrist and psychologist. The psychiatrist's diagnoses were listed as major depressive disorder, alcohol abuse, cannabis abuse, and borderline personality disorder. Their psychologist had stated that, at the time of the homicide, Patrick Ford had had no control over his rational thinking, judgment, or behavior. This news did not change my opinion at all about the defendant. I had no reason to believe and could not accept their view. Mike then stated that our prosecution team's psychiatrist had reviewed all the defense team's mental health evaluation reports related to the defendant and had begun her own evaluation. She had already seen Patrick Ford one time in Cook County Jail and would visit him at least a few more times to complete her evaluation. My anticipation built with this knowledge that soon a decision would be made as to the direction of this case, trial or no trial.

As I mentioned earlier, the methodical process of psychiatric and psychological evaluations is slow. As aggravating as it was to wait, I had no problem with our prosecution team's psychiatrist taking her time and being as thorough as necessary to make an informed decision. Of course, I prayed she would find him legally sane and able to stand trial for murder. The decision on whether to continue with a trial after the defendant was evaluated by psychiatrists from both sides was yet to be determined. Now we had to wait for the prosecution team's psychiatric and psychological reports to see how the case would proceed.

While it was a challenge for me at times to ignore worries and thoughts about what might happen, I was pretty successful in not obsessing over the evaluators' diagnoses, whether there would be a trial, or what the outcome would be. My work during this healing journey was to let go of things I could not control. Nothing positive could result from letting the what-ifs consume me.

CHAPTER 23

AN EMOTIONAL SHIFT

How had I survived this grueling, drawn-out court process in the case against Dana's accused murderer? One thing I had been told by our prosecutor early on was that this would most likely be a long court case. This journey brought many reflections and lessons I would never have expected or predicted.

I realized early on that I needed to know as much as possible about what had happened to Dana, even as some family members tried to change my mind. They loved me, and they were worried about what hearing the gruesome details might do to my fragile emotional state. Yet again, I had chosen to do what was right for me even though it may have been wrong for anyone else. And I prayed my God would take care of me no matter what happened.

Eventually, as the weeks and years went by and I had attended almost every court hearing, I had been able to let go and accept that we would never get all the answers. By then, in my healing process, it no longer held as much importance to me. This revelation was stunning to me at the time and was a miraculous emotional shift in my healing process.

CHAPTER 24

HEIGHTENED ANTICIPATION

Now, as 2009 ended, I prayed this case against Patrick Ford would be over sometime in 2010. During the last three status hearings of 2009, not much of interest to me occurred except that I would get an update about the status of the psychiatric evaluations. Aware that the prosecution's psychiatrist was completing her evaluations as 2009 was winding down, I took the time to ask Mike to explain a bit about the trial process. Always wishing to be as prepared as possible, I wanted to send information to my siblings so they could decide whether they would attend if there was a trial.

Things moved quickly after the new year of 2010. In January 2010, our prosecutor was informed that the prosecution team's psychiatric and psychological reports were complete. The psychiatrist stated that Patrick Ford's diagnoses (at the time of the alleged offense) were cannabis abuse, alcohol abuse, and personality disorder. The prosecution's psychologist stated that Patrick had been legally sane at the time of the alleged offense. He was not experiencing signs or symptoms of a mental disease or defect at the time of the alleged offense that would have made him incapable of understanding he was doing something criminal. The pretrial discovery phase was finally complete when Mike turned over the prosecution's mental health evaluation report to the defense attorney in February 2010.

At a status hearing in early March 2010, before our case was called before the judge, the defense attorney informed our prosecutor, Mike, that he had discussed our forty-year offer with Patrick Ford during the prior month. Our offer had been declined. During the conversation this day, just between the two attorneys, the defense attorney asked if we would consider a thirty-year offer, to which Mike replied, "No." Our prosecutor then informed the defense attorney that our final offer (agreed to by Joe, Sarah, and me in advance), if his client was serious about accepting an offer and taking responsibility for murdering Dana, would be for him to plead "guilty but mentally ill" with a thirty-five-year prison sentence. This went back and forth a few times with the defense attorney then asking for a thirty-three-year sentence that was not accepted, and finally a thirty-four-year sentence that was not accepted. I had no idea all this back-and-forth had transpired before the status hearing even began. Once Patrick Ford was brought into the courtroom, the defense attorney told the judge he would visit his client over the weekend to discuss our final offer, and then give Patrick five days to consider. The next court date was set for a week later, March 11, 2010.

After the status hearing was over, I met with Mike in his office. It was then he explained what had taken place before the status hearing had begun. I was grateful he had refused to negotiate to a lesser sentence. Mike also explained what might occur at this next court date. It was still the right of the defendant to choose whether he would accept our offer or go to trial. If Patrick did not accept our offer at the next court date, a trial date would be set, probably six to eight weeks from then. If the accused murderer accepted the offer, Mike would then have to give the judge factual reasons to justify our thirty-five-year sentence and give some background about the facts of the case. He wanted to prepare me for the fact that I would hear some of the gruesome details he would need to present that day. So now we waited.

The day after that status hearing, I had another discussion with our prosecutor. I had had more time to process all I had heard the day before. I could not help but wonder if next week would be the "sentencing" of Patrick Ford, so to speak, if he did indeed accept our offer. As March 11 drew nearer, I had several questions for Mike: Did Mike think the defense attorney would know what Patrick's decision was before March 11? If so, would the defense attorney call our prosecutor to give us a heads-up? Mike had no answers for me. Would Mike let us know, if he did find out ahead of time, what he had decided? Yes, our prosecutor would let us know.

Knowing this next status hearing could be the end of Patrick Ford's criminal case, my mind was working feverishly now, obsessing over the what-ifs. To avoid being consumed by questions I couldn't answer, I was determined instead to focus on anything I might have some control over that day. Certainly, I would want to give our small family and a few friends the opportunity to be there with us for Dana and for closure, if they chose to do so. It was time to let them know March 11 might be the end of this criminal case.

Mike and I had discussed months earlier about Sarah and me composing our victim impact statements. A victim impact statement is a personal account, either an oral or written statement, that all victims as well as survivors of deceased victims are entitled to make regarding the personal impact of a crime in financial, physical, and emotional terms. Generally, if there is a trial and the verdict is guilty, the victims and the survivors of crime victims can present these statements during a sentencing hearing. We had written our impact statements to eventually be read in court if there was a trial at some point and Patrick Ford was found guilty. Mike had explained to me back then that victim impact statements were not usually read in the courtroom when the defendant had accepted an offer to plead guilty. This decision would be at the discretion of the judge.

Now that there was a possibility Patrick Ford might accept our offer on March 11, whether we would be able to read our impact statements was forefront in my mind. I so desperately wanted to read mine in the courtroom that day. I yearned to describe who Dana had been to everyone in that courtroom as a living, breathing person and not just a murder victim, and to relay how our world had been shattered forever.

Clearly, as if it were just yesterday, I remember a sense of peace washing over me as I reflected on what decision our judge might make. I truly respected our judge, as I had watched him through the years making many difficult decisions on such a variety of cases and the crimes they involved. None of the cases I had heard him presiding over were as violent as our case. Still, our judge surprised me many times when I thought an accused offender standing before him would be sent straight to jail, but was given a chance at probation first. But make no mistake—if that accused offender was seen back in the judge's courtroom for breaking parole or committing another crime, there would be no leniency. I found him to be fair but tough, compassionate and understanding, but certainly never a pushover. I had attended almost every court status hearing starting in April 2008, just short of two years ago. I had sat quietly and respectfully, listening to the proceedings not only for Patrick Ford's status hearings but also for those cases called before ours. I had never caused any kind of disturbance in the courtroom. So, when it came time for our judge to decide whether to let one or both of us read our impact statements to everyone who would be in that courtroom on March 11, I trusted he would allow us to have our say. I hoped I was correct.

On March 8, 2010, I received a phone call from our prosecutor. Mike informed me the judge had been told about our offer and he had approved it. Our judge had not disappointed me. He would allow our two impact statements to be read! Mike also told me that Patrick Ford, in three days at the next court hearing, would plead "guilty but mentally ill" to first-degree murder with a prison sentence of thirty-five years. However, Mike tempered my excitement and relief with the explanation that, until we heard the defendant accept our offer in the courtroom, we should contain our excitement. The defendant could change his mind again before that date. All I could do was pray and wait to hear the final decision.

CHAPTER 25

MARCH 11, 2010

March 11, 2010 finally arrived. I experienced a plethora of emotions that morning as we prepared to leave for the Criminal Court Building, hopefully for the last time. My sister, Cindy, who had driven from Wisconsin the night before, as well as one of my dearest girlfriends, Timi, would accompany Joe and me to court. Thank God for these two special women in my life who could help keep me calm and distracted from the many thoughts running through my head. Sarah would meet us at the courthouse with a few friends. I just wanted to hold her close as we sat through this unreal plea-agreement hearing. Joe's sister, Linda, along with her daughter and son-in-law, would drive down separately and meet us there as well. With an extreme sense of anxiety that Patrick Ford would change his mind at the last minute, a sense of anticipation that this nightmare might actually be over after today, and a sense of hope that I would get some closure and see justice served this day, we began our somber journey down to the Cook County Criminal Court Building.

Once our group was escorted into the courtroom, Sarah, Joe, and I were seated right in the front row. Our victim specialist, Pam, was sitting behind me. Sarah and I were particularly anxious, holding tight to each other's hands and each wondering if we would be able to get through our victim impact statements when the time came. As I had gone to court religiously the prior two years, I had heard nothing about the defendant having shame or sorrow for what he did. Therefore, my unbending conviction going into this plea-agreement hearing was that Patrick Ford did not care about what he had done, nor would he show any remorse when I read my impact statement. This firm conviction was centered on all my own theories based on the facts as I knew them, as well as the fact that I could never comprehend why he had taken my most precious daughter from me.

I was feeling extremely anxious and nauseated as we waited to begin. Would anything go wrong and change the anticipated outcome my family so desperately waited for? This plea was the absolute best-case scenario we could have hoped for. Patrick Ford would be put away in prison for a long time with no chance of parole or appeals. We would avoid having to sit through a trial where a jury could convict him of a lesser crime and he could get out in much less time! Less likely but possible, we would avoid him being found "not guilty by reason of insanity," where he could conceivably be released from an institution for the criminally insane by a court order at some date in the future. So, as our group sat there waiting for the proceedings to begin, I could only hope and pray all would go as planned.

When all necessary parties were present—the judge, the two attorneys, the defendant, the clerk, and the official shorthand reporter—the case began. The judge started by asking the prosecution attorney, Mike, and the defense attorney to identify themselves. Then the judge asked the defense attorney to tell him what terms the defendant had agreed to.

The defense attorney stated in the public court record, "With the Court's approval, after a finding of guilty but mentally ill, a sentence would be imposed of 35 [sic] years."

The judge then questioned our prosecution attorney, Mike, to make sure he was accepting Patrick Ford's plea, which our prosecutor agreed to. At that point, the judge questioned Patrick at length to ensure he understood the charge against him. Once the judge was confident he understood, he specifically asked him, "How do you plead in this charge, guilty or not guilty?"

To which the defendant answered, "Guilty."

Now the judge explained that Mr. Ford would be giving up certain rights by pleading guilty to this crime. He would be giving up the right to plead not guilty and have a trial by a jury of his peers. The jury would decide guilt or innocence after they listened to all the evidence, and decide whether the State had proven the charge against him beyond a reasonable doubt. The defendant would also be giving up the right to a second type of trial, a bench trial, where the judge would preside over the matter. The judge, instead of a jury, would make that same determination whether the State had proven the charge against him beyond a reasonable doubt.

After giving all this information, he questioned Patrick, "Do you understand the rights you're giving up by pleading guilty today, sir?"

To which the defendant answered, "Yes, sir."

The judge then explained the range of sentencing possibilities to ensure Patrick also understood those conditions. Finally, Patrick denied there had been any force, threats, or bribes to get him to plead guilty. He agreed he was pleading guilty of his own free will and that he was satisfied with his representation. Once the judge was confident all had been followed to the letter of the law, he requested that the prosecution attorney justify a thirty-five-year prison sentence.

Our prosecutor, Mike, was required to describe the details of Dana's murder as well as evidence that would have been presented if there had been a trial: "Judge, on August 18, 2007 at approximately 7:00 o'clock [sic] p.m. . . . in Chicago, Cook County, Illinois, the evidence in this case would show that Patrick Ford inflicted injuries to the victim, Dana Mangi, which resulted in her death."

Mike went on to specifically describe how Mr. Ford had killed her. Mike explained that evidence would have been presented from the Cook County Medical Examiner's Office, and that the doctor would have testified as to how the body had been found and the specific causes of her death. Mike stated the evidence would have shown during a trial that Patrick Ford was the individual who had inflicted these injuries. He had placed a 911 call on the early morning of August 19, 2007, stating he had killed someone the day before.

There would have been testimony from the lead detective that he had had a conversation with the defendant at the hospital and advised him of his Miranda warnings, after which Mr. Ford admitted he had inflicted the injuries. Finally, there would have been testimony from the psychiatrist and psychologist for the prosecution that, after reviewing the reports from the defense experts, would have given their expert opinions within a reasonable degree of medical and psychiatric certainty that Patrick Ford was legally sane at the time of the offense. Mike then read directly from the prosecution psychiatrist's report describing in graphic detail how the defendant had killed my precious daughter.

One detail I heard and visualized, in that brief report, was a complete shock to me, taking my breath away and piercing my wounded heart once again. Our victim specialist, Pam, leaned in to me and gave me a tissue as the tears rolled down my face. Even though I had been told most of the details long ago, I was now in the same position as my family and friends here with me today. I could only imagine how they all were impacted by the brutality of what we had just heard, and my heart also hurt for each of them. That statement was the only bit of information Mike shared with the judge that I had not already heard in my two years of going to court. I could only pray I would pull myself together enough to read my impact statement.

The judge then made his decision: "Let the record reflect the defendant understands the nature and charge against him, the possible penalties of the law, his rights under the law. I find the plea to be free, voluntarily and intelligently entered into. I believe there is a factual basis for the plea. There will be a finding of guilty in this matter."

He went on to say he had perused all of the psychiatric and psychological reports from the defense and from the prosecution. "I will also make the following finding: That while I do not believe that stipulated testimony is such that would indicate the defendant was legally insane at the time of the occurrence, I do believe that he was suffering from a mental illness, and the mental illness as defined by statute I believe based on the stipulated testimony exists which is a substantial disorder of thought, mood or behavior which afflicted the person at the time of the commission of the offense in which impaired that person's judgment but not to the extent that he is unable to appreciate the wrongfulness of his behavior."

The time had now arrived for Sarah and me to come forward to read our victim impact statements. I took a deep breath as our prosecutor announced, "The People call Barb Mangi."

As I shakily walked into the glassed-in courtroom, past the defense table, and approached the judge, he instructed me, "You can have a seat at the counsel table."

I took my seat, which gave me a direct view of Patrick Ford straight ahead of me. I avoided looking at him, fearing I would break down. Instead I focused on looking past him to my family and friends sitting on the other side of the glass. The judge was to my right, so I could not see him as Mike began examining me as required. I had to state my full name and spell the last name, and verify that I was the mother of Dana Mangi, that I had prepared an impact statement for purposes of court, and that I had a copy of my statement with me. The judge asked the defense attorney if he had any objection to me reading that statement, to which he replied, "No." And so, trying to keep my emotions in check, I shakily began:

"Dana's short life and her unconditional love for me have given me a joy beyond measure. She was a loving, caring, kind-hearted, empathetic daughter with a great love of life. What an amazing gift from God I was given in watching her develop and blossom into a unique young woman who was beautiful inside as well as out, one who had a strong character, a fighting spirit, a magnetic and funny personality and an infectious laugh that is forever etched into my memory. Together as we journeyed through her many struggles, I witnessed her inner strength and determination over and over again.

"One of Dana's graduate school professors shared with me that they often talked about her family. She observed that Dana depended on our counsel and support and that there was no question that we were the source of her strength. As in any family, the 25 [sic] years we all shared were not perfect but we were ALWAYS there for each other. We were very close and enjoyed spending time together; watching movies, vacationing, going to baseball games, just hanging out, being silly, and laughing a lot. And, unlike some families, that didn't change even as the girls became adults. Dana always made the effort to stay in touch with her many aunts, uncles and cousins who lived far from us. One of my sisters [Sue] wrote to me after Dana's murder saying, 'Dana was the one who would email to wish us a Happy Thanksgiving or Merry Christmas. She was the one who always signed it "Love you guys." In her short life, she had an impact on many. We were blessed to have known her and loved her.'

"Dana has an older sister, Sarah. Being the 'baby', Dana took her job as the annoying little sister very seriously. My daughters were typical sisters, alternately fighting and playing together. But as they got older they became closer and were each other's advocate and protector. My heart overflowed with love and pride when I saw each of them being so proud of the other, supporting each other and wanting each other to find joy, happiness and love in their lives. They truly learned so much from each other, even though they may not have admitted it. I saw it and I heard from each of them about their devotion to the other.

"Dana never lacked friends. Quite the contrary, from the time she was a young, school-aged child, her 'bubbly' and friendly personality drew others to her. She was one of those friends you felt like you had known forever, even from the beginning of a budding friendship. Whoever she embraced as her friend, she gave 200% [sic] of herself. She trusted those who she cared about and when they hurt her, there always seemed to be room in her heart for forgiveness and for giving them another chance.

"In addition to being extremely smart and a tenacious student all the way through graduate school, Dana participated in a variety of extracurricular activities including variety shows, choir, a dance troupe, an ice skating team, a high school softball team, a diver on a swim team, a leader in her college sorority and a volunteer at a clinic for the underprivileged during graduate school. However, it was the exciting discovery during college of her passion for improving the lives of animals and their owners that defined her career path towards veterinary medicine. Dana was denied admittance twice into vet school but, being a woman of courage and persistence, she would not let go of her dream. At age 25 [sic], after completing a Master's degree in Biomedical Science to advance her knowledge of medical sciences, she finally realized her dream and was accepted into the University of Minnesota's College of Veterinary Medicine. Dana was so proud and exuded a confidence and sense of purpose that was almost palpable. My heart was bursting with happiness, pride and joy for her! I couldn't wait to travel this journey with her. However, just two weeks before starting vet school, on August 18, 2007 my precious daughter's life was brutally ripped away.

"Our nightmare and hell on earth began early on the morning of August 19. I don't believe there are words to truly describe my feelings when I heard the cruel, shocking words, 'Dana was murdered,' that morning. It had taken all of my strength to remain calm throughout the previous night when Dana didn't come home and to tell myself there was some reasonable explanation. She was a daughter who texted or called if she was going to be late or her plans changed. I was in shock, dazed, stunned, feeling an immeasurable, unrelenting pain like part of my heart was being ripped out. All of us who loved Dana had a piece of ourselves brutally ripped away that day. We are ALL victims. It was incomprehensible to me, and still is almost three years later, how a person could do this to another human being, especially to my beautiful Dana. Who? Why? How was this possible? One of my horrible memories of that morning and one of my biggest regrets is having to call Sarah, alone in the city, and tell her that her sister had been murdered so she wouldn't see it on the early morning news. Even now I am still tormented by that unimaginable trauma inflicted on her and by the thought of her being alone before a friend could get there to comfort her while we were on our way downtown.

"It haunts me and fills me with such an intense pain to think of Dana suffering, terrified and defenseless, and me not being there to comfort her, hold her and tell her how much I love her. It kills me to know that she died alone. To know that my child was strangled to death and then stabbed so many times has inflicted a devastating emotional trauma that will last a lifetime. It cannot be mercifully erased from my mind, ever. The deep sadness of what I have lost overwhelms me at times. It is in these darkest moments, when my heart feels like it's breaking, that I grieve that I will never again be able to touch her, hug her, kiss her, hear her beautiful voice and laughter, see her smile or hear her call me 'mama', even at age 25 [sic]! I will never again be able to comfort her, to be her cheerleader, her protector, her counselor, her mom. I'll never be able to walk with her as she becomes a veterinarian, as she falls in love with someone who truly deserves her, as she gets married, has children. That future has cruelly been stolen from me. On another level, because of this selfish act, this heinous crime, my fear of losing my loving, caring, beautiful daughter Sarah is sometimes still so intense that, when I go to that place, I can't breathe. In those times, I pray that I won't have to live to lose her too.

"I know firsthand what a gift it is to have siblings to share my life's joyful and unbelievably painful moments with since I come from a very large family. I am filled with a deep sadness for Sarah because her life has been shattered and her dreams altered forever in losing her sister and her only sibling. I grieve for their lost opportunity to share in each other's lives and families. It breaks my heart to see Sarah's pain and heartbreak. I so desperately wish I could take the pain away for her and protect her from this hellish nightmare. But all I can do is be there with her as we walk this unwanted journey together.

"Dana has an amazing group of close friends, many whom I have known for years. The saying, 'The company one keeps is a reflection of who they are,' more than holds true. The love that

Dana had for others is just as evident in her closest friends. We continue to keep in touch and I love to be around them, to be a part of their lives. We share a bond and it makes me feel close to Dana when I'm with them. My heart hurts for them because they loved Dana too. For all of these young people in Dana's life; her sister, her cousins, her friends and her classmates, the world they knew changed forever that horrible day. I grieve for all that they have lost and keep them all close in my heart. Because of one person's senseless, violent act so many people whose lives Dana touched have been emotionally traumatized.

"As a family, we are healing each in our own time and in our own way. I lost my mother suddenly at a young age and my dad died just 6 [sic] weeks before Dana was murdered. As painful and sad as those two losses were to me, they don't even come close to the emptiness and overwhelming sadness I've been feeling since Dana was killed. Losing my own child is the worst kind of pain I think I will ever have to endure. And yet there is still a real sadness about not having had much of a chance to grieve the loss of my dad because of Dana's death following his so closely. My husband, Joe, and I deal with our grief very differently. He grieves in a very private way. But for me to survive this indescribable tragedy, I need to be able to talk about Dana and to keep her memory alive for all of us who loved her. Hopefully, some day Joe and I will be able to share our memories of our life with Dana, laughing together, crying together and healing together. I try not to dwell on the horror of Dana's murder, but on the sweet memories of my life with her that will be in my heart as long as I live. NO ONE, not even Dana's murderer, can take that away from me! I DO want justice and believe that people must suffer the consequences of their actions. I believe that if we have to live in the aftermath of what Patrick Ford has done, then so should he. But I refuse to live a life full of hate and revenge. That would only eat me up inside and hold me back from healing. I know that I will continue to experience waves of sadness during my life, but I choose to focus on God's most precious gift of Dana's life and her love for me.

"My life is richer because Dana lived. So much of me is made of what I learned from her. My heart is overflowing with pride in all that she was, in all that she accomplished in her short life, and in all that we dreamed together that she would become. My cherished daughter left a truly remarkable legacy, evidenced by all that has been accomplished in her name. I am blessed and honored to have called Dana my daughter and I will strive to make a difference in this world in her name."

During my statement, I became teary eyed and my voice quivered a few times, but overall, I was able to keep it together. While I spoke, I concentrated on looking to my family and friends as well as to our prosecutor, Mike. Even though I truly did not believe Patrick Ford would be moved by what I was saying, I desperately needed him to hear how his actions had devastated all of us and rocked our world when he had taken Dana's life. Still, I purposely avoided glancing at him as I read this statement, thinking I might totally fall apart. On the other hand, as I was walking back to the gallery where my family was sitting, I found the courage to look him in the eye for a second or two. In that moment, I wanted him to see my pain and my heartbreak.

Now it was Sarah's turn. Focused, she rose and was escorted into the inner courtroom to take a seat next to the judge. Watching her, I was both so proud of her courage and so sad for us that our lives had come to this moment. And she began . . .

"Dana was my little sister and my best friend. She was the one person I always assumed would be with me to enjoy the moments of happiness and celebration and to face the moments of sadness and despair. I might have been the older sister, but I learned so much from her. Dana had a gift for loving others with all her heart, touching the lives of those around her, and always giving 200% [*sic*] of herself. Her smile was contagious and her laugh infectious. She was beautiful and smart, and I was proud to be her sister.

"The twenty-five years we had together as a family, as sisters, and as friends were not perfect, but they were full of love and happiness. Our family, the four of us, were very close. We laughed a lot, took fun family vacations, and, no matter what, we always had each other. I wouldn't give up those 25 [sic] years for anything. Not even to take away the pain that will forever be in my heart because she is gone. There is no pain as terrible as losing someone you love. Seeing Dana's lifeless twenty-five year old [sic] body in a casket that my mom and I had to pick out. Following Dana's casket down the aisle of our church during her funeral. And watching my dad cry with the sadness of not being able to protect his baby girl. These things are heart-wrenching, and at times they still can take my breath away when I think of them. This is the pain I will live with forever.

"I miss Dana so much. I miss talking to her and hugging her. I miss her clammy hands and feet. I miss the stupid text messages we used to send back and forth. I miss laughing with her and hearing her wonderful, carefree laugh. I miss 'saving' her when something went wrong and she needed her big sister. I miss being a big sister.

"For the life of me I still cannot comprehend that all these things are over. That she won't be around to laugh with me as we get old together. That she won't be there when I get married or have children. That my children will never know her. And that I won't get to watch her do all the things I dreamed she'd do ... vet school, marriage, lots of children. Dana was supposed to start vet school at the University of Minnesota just weeks after she was taken from us. She had spent the last three years of her life working toward that dream. Dana taught me what it meant to be persistent. Despite getting rejected by vet schools two years in a row, Dana worked hard to enhance her qualifications by completing a master's program and working at several veterinary clinics. When she finally got accepted, she was so excited to finally pursue her dream. Dana loved animals. She would have made a wonderful vet.

"I cannot believe that it has been almost three years since we lost her. I still talk to her in my head. I don't understand life without her. I miss her terribly. So much has happened in my life since she died. I want so much to tell her everything. I want to tell her how scared I am to live the rest of my life without her, as an only child. I want to tell her how alone I feel some days, and how I wish she were here. She was my sister and my best friend. She was supposed to be with me forever.

"My life was changed forever the day my sister was murdered. It is still hard for me to say this word out loud. My sister, my best friend, the one constant in my life, was taken from me forever. I wasn't given the chance to protect her or to protest. I went to bed with a sister, and I woke up the next morning an only child. This is my life now. Patrick Ford did this. Patrick Ford took my sister from everyone who loved her forever. Patrick Ford cut Dana's promising young life short and took everything from her—her hopes, her dreams. The impact of his actions will live with me forever, as a hole in my heart, a sadness in my soul, and a terror in my mind."

I had already read her statement more than once, and it had broken my heart each time. But seeing her up there, so vulnerable, so sad, and so broken, hearing her voice and her pain as she read her statement to the court, affected me in a way I never expected. Once again, I was overcome with such a heart-wrenching sadness for Sarah as she spoke about all she had lost, and about how alone she felt. Like when I had found out Dana had been murdered, I felt as if yet another piece of my heart was being ripped apart as I witnessed Sarah's immeasurable pain and sadness. Maddeningly, there was nothing I could do to take away her pain and suffering. I felt inadequate knowing all I could do was be there for her and love her. Once she was finished, Sarah stepped down from the counsel table and returned to the gallery to sit next to me.

At this point in the hearing, our prosecutor rested his case. The judge and the two attorneys addressed and settled a few other legal matters to do with the case against Patrick Ford. Then, our judge began a short conversation with Patrick, which I never saw coming.

The Court [this is our judge speaking]: "Is there anything you want to tell me before I impose the sentence?"

The Defendant: "Yes, sir. Shall I stand?"

The Court: "Wherever you are comfortable."
The Defendant: "It is okay if I address the Mangi family briefly?"
The Court: "Yes."

I was completely and utterly stunned at this turn of events. This was not something we had been told might happen ahead of time, so it came as a complete shock. Patrick Ford was sitting with his defense team directly in front of us on the other side of the glass. He stood up, turned around, and moved over to face Sarah and me. There was probably no more than three to four feet between us. Stunned, I focused on his face as he began to speak to us.

CHAPTER 26

LIFE CHANGER

Early in their investigation, the prosecutor and the lead detective had told me that, in his confession, Patrick Ford stated he did not know why he had killed Dana. But I had never heard from them that he expressed sorrow for what he had done. In addition, I had heard from some of Dana's Loyola University friends about a few incidents between Patrick and Dana years ago in college, as well as between him and some of Dana's friends. Because of these reasons, for the entire time I had been going to court, almost two years by this time, I had only thought of him as someone who did not care about what he had done to Dana and to all of us who loved her. Since I had heard nothing to the contrary all this time, my conviction was based on my own limited knowledge about the defendant, my own theories based on the facts as I knew them, and on the fact that I could never comprehend why the defendant had taken my most precious daughter from me. Hence, that ongoing struggle within me to forgive him had never been resolved. Yet I had continued praying to God to help me forgive throughout these years, even though I still had no idea how that could ever happen. My healing process had been continuing every single day, but my heart was still hardened, not yet ready to forgive this young man. As I said, I steeled myself this day with the idea that Patrick Ford did not care about what he had done and would not show any sorrow or remorse during the plea-agreement hearing. How shockingly wrong I was!

The Defendant: "I'm so sorry. I know that my words can't help you. And I took something from you that I can never give back, but I swear to you that I did not mean to do what I did and if there was anything I can do or say to take away your pain, I would. I promise you that. And all I can do is keep you in my prayers forever and let you know that I'm just so, so sorry."

As I sat there listening to him, stunned, I could see him clearly for the very first time because he was so close to us, and I heard him loud and clear. I saw the pain in his eyes and heard the quivering in his voice as emotionally he spoke to us, looking us straight in the eye. In that moment, the words he said evoked a sense of compassion in me and, shockingly, sadness for him—for what his life would be because of what he had done. Then I focused my attention on the judge as he addressed the courtroom.

The Court: "I think it's probably a given for people that work in the criminal justice system to acknowledge, if they are being truthful, that sometimes we get pretty cold and pretty unemotional about a lot of crimes that occur. There is [sic] a lot of things that come through the courtrooms: there may be drug cases, there may be gun cases, there may be quote unquote, 'victimless crimes,' and we also have violent crimes. And what all of us realize, particularly after listening to the facts of cases and listening to, quite frankly, some heart wrenching victim impact statements, that the consequences of crime go far beyond the defendant, they go far beyond the victim, and they reach out to a different level and ripple out like waves into the sea.

"As a judge, I have to sentence you. I have to come up with a sentence that's fair and just and not only just for you, Mr. Ford, but also just for the community and to take into consideration the circumstances surrounding the crime and the crime that was actually committed. For the life of me, I don't understand this, I cannot understand this, nor will I ever understand this, nor do I think anyone in this courtroom will ever understand what you did that day, why you did it, and the consequences of your actions. There was [sic] extensive interviews done of you, there was extensive testing done of you. I've read and perused the medical and psychiatric summaries and the test results, and again, this doesn't answer any questions to me.

"After much, I assume, negotiation between the defense and the prosecution, they came up with a recommendation to present for me and obviously I'm free to accept that recommendation or reject that recommendation. After listening to all the evidence here, listening to and knowing what I know about the facts of the case now, and also knowing about your medical and your psychiatric background, I do feel that this is a just sentence. I also know what you know right now that you just stated, Mr. Ford, that whatever sentence I could give you, whether it be 80 [sic] years, 120 [sic] years, life in prison, could not turn the hands of time back and bring Dana Mangi back to her loved ones. Unfortunately, that's the reality, the hard and cold reality of your acts.

"Because I do believe this is a fair and just sentence, I will go along with a sentence of 35 [sic] years in the Illinois Department of Corrections. Because you have been found guilty but mentally ill, you will serve that sentence in the Illinois Department of Corrections. However, you will be first transported to a penitentiary with a psychiatric hospital and psychiatric ward and you will be treated until a time they see fit to release you to general population in the Illinois Department of Corrections.

". . . Obviously, besides sentencing you to 35 [sic] years in jail, for the rest of your life you will be dealing with your conscience, and what you did and the consequences of what you did, and that's obviously a self-imposed sentence. That's something that no court, no defendant's family, or no victim's family can impose upon you."

Having finished this statement, the judge addressed Patrick with a few more legal matters to ensure he understood everything to do with his sentencing. With no other questions from the attorneys, this plea agreement ended. Our prosecutor, Mike, gave us the opportunity to meet with him and ask any additional questions, once he completed all he needed to do for this proceeding. We were ushered back to a conference room to wait for him before we departed for the last time after two and a half years of awaiting justice!

While sitting in the conference room, my mind was going a mile a minute. I had had no time to process these unexpected feelings I had felt as Patrick had spoken to us because the court hearing had continued with the statement from our judge. But now I felt like my head was going to implode with all my traitorous thoughts whirling around. I was in such a painful, confused state that I could not even begin to imagine how I was going to come to grips with all my thoughts and feelings.

Oh my God, oh my God! How can I feel compassion and sadness for this person who killed my beloved Dana? What kind of mother am I? How can I live with myself for being such a traitor to her memory? I cannot tell anyone what I'm feeling! What will they think of me? What am I going to do now?

Once Mike and Pam, our victim specialist, came down and talked with us in the conference room, answering any questions anyone had, in gratitude we thanked them for all they had done for us through these past two and a half years. Mike and I would meet again in the future, whenever I was ready to do so, to go over any other questions I may still have about this case. These wonderful people had carried me through this entire process, and I would miss their guidance, their compassion, and their kindness. We had been blessed with an incredible team of professionals from beginning to end—from the lead detective, Detective Ed; to our prosecutor, Mike; our victim specialist, Pam; and, finally, our judge. I realize we might be the exception in this regard, but I am so thankful for the way I was treated and nurtured through my time in the court system.

The lead detective on our case, Detective Ed, was not how I had envisioned a Chicago cop. Detective Ed was the one who had called us that horrible morning. He had been my first source of information about the case. He had given me his cell phone number and told me to call him with any questions that surfaced. He had always answered my questions with compassion and respect.

I had wanted to meet Detective Ed and thank him in person for all he had done to help me. So, after one of our status hearings, I had asked our prosecutor, Mike, if I would ever be able to. One day, Detective Ed had surprised me by taking time out of his day to meet me in Mike's office after our status hearing. When I had entered the room, Detective Ed had hugged me and told me how sorry he was for us and for having to deliver that news by phone. I greatly appreciated that kind and considerate gesture, which I will never forget. He and his partner were in the courtroom at the plea agreement and waited for us afterward. Again, he gave me a hug, asked me if I still had his cell phone number, and told me to call him anytime if I had any more questions for him. Joe, Sarah, and everyone else got to meet these two detectives who were so affected by Dana's murder.

Our prosecutor, Mike, was an amazing man who took our feelings and wishes into account whenever the law allowed him to do so. I experienced his real sense of compassion, even though he saw some of the worst crimes at the Criminal Court Building every day. He had been my source of information throughout these last two and a half years and had treated me with respect and kindness at every turn. He never seemed to be annoyed with me for all my questions (even though he may have been), and he understood my need to get as many answers as possible for my healing. He would continue to work with me, now that this case was over, to go through whatever I wanted to see of the case he had put together, as the law permitted.

Our victim specialist, Pam, was warm, caring, comforting, and knowledgeable about the process. She had patiently helped me understand things that were going on in the courtroom during the status hearings. When I had brought in photos and albums of Dana living and enjoying her life, Pam had always shown interest and asked me questions about the photos. It takes a strong person to do the work she did every day in her job to help grieving families get through the court process. She was protective and observant for us on that day in court. During the proceeding (I believe it was when I was reading my impact statement), she had reprimanded a defense lawyer who was still in the courtroom arguing with a client. She had told them to leave the courtroom so that those who were with me could hear my statement.

I did not think our judge could surprise me any more than he had done countless times as I had sat in the courtroom these last two years. But his statements that day had touched me deeply. I believe the judge acknowledged the impact of what Patrick Ford had done. He had spoken about the senselessness and his lack of understanding how it happened as well as addressing the pain we have been living with and will continue to live with forever. I had been aware of the judge searching for a tissue as I had been speaking, but I had never moved my gaze to him. However, as Sarah had been reading, he had been overcome with emotion. I will be forever grateful to him for his unwavering compassion and understanding at allowing us to read our impact statements. That had been at his discretion. And on a deeper level, I am profoundly moved that he had been totally engaged as Sarah had poured out her heart.

As Joe, Cindy, Timi, and I drove back out to the suburbs, I left a piece of myself at the Criminal Court Building. It was challenging for me to let that go. Sarah verbalized this years later in such a beautiful, yet bittersweet way when she said, "It was your connection to Dana. While you were doing this, you were still walking with her, but this is where the road ended . . . that is its own kind of pain, even though we got what we wanted."

It was so difficult for me to believe we were truly done and for me to comprehend, in the moment, that my spirit had been set free. Never again would I have the next court status hearing in the back of my mind. I needed time and quiet to truly process everything that had occurred. I had been changed forever during this court process, but I had yet to admit that or understand how it had affected me.

CHAPTER 27

WHERE DO I GO FROM HERE?

Returning home that day, once Joe and I were alone, we did not discuss what had transpired except that we were both satisfied with the outcome. Then I retreated into the privacy of my thoughts. That afternoon, I was so horribly torn. I was having a huge internal struggle, one I felt I could not discuss with anyone! In my heart, I felt Patrick Ford had told the truth rather than saying what we'd wanted to hear. But, in my mind, I fought with feeling that I was betraying Dana and my family if I accepted his words. I felt as if I were going crazy with this dilemma, and I felt so alone. As much as I had always felt better sharing my feelings with those closest to me during this entire two-and-a-half-year ordeal, now I could not share this with anyone, certainly not with Joe, and not even with my own daughter. I did not want to hurt them.

Sarah phoned me early that same evening. She had left the courthouse earlier to go back into the city for work, so she and I had not been able to discuss Patrick Ford's address to us. Without warning, Sarah blurted out how she had felt while he was talking. Unbelievably, she had had the same reaction as me! She was scared I might be shattered by her confession. But that fear was overridden by her desperate need to share what she was feeling with her mom, if for no other reason than to discuss how to deal with her raw emotion from these events. As I listened, I was so overwhelmed with no longer feeling alone in this ordeal, so awed by the mystery of how we could each have gotten to this place, and so amazingly grateful to have such a powerful emotional connection with this daughter I loved more than life itself. Unlike me, Sarah was incredibly brave. I am humbled and so blessed she felt comfortable enough in our relationship to confide in me. Hanging up, I realized a huge weight had been lifted from me. Now, Sarah's most remarkable revelation gave me the courage to begin to sort through all my swirling thoughts and feelings. If nothing else, at least I no longer felt alone.

Within a few days of Sarah's revelation to me, I was startled once again. My girlfriend, Timi, who had been at the plea-agreement hearing, admitted to me she had felt similar compassion toward Patrick as he had spoken to us. Unbelievably, she had no idea yet what my reaction had been. What bravery she exhibited in possibly losing me as a longtime friend! Knowing I now had two strong and brave allies who understood my unbelievable reaction gave me such comfort as I continued to sort out my feelings.

To be honest, it took several days for me to process all that I had heard and experienced at the plea-agreement hearing. Patrick Ford's request that day was a defining moment for me. Even if he had not asked to speak to our family, I probably would have gotten some closure because of his sentence. But I would still have been haunted with not knowing whether he had felt any sorrow for what he had done. He did not have to address us that day. The sentence was final; he had nothing to gain. He did not have to turn around, face us, and look us in the eye as he spoke, but he had chosen to do so. He had acknowledged what he had done to Dana and to all of us who love her.

I struggled with knowing I had felt that compassion and sadness for him. I felt traitorous for these feelings, wondering how I could feel that way toward the person who had killed my precious Dana. And yet, it was too late to take back what I had felt in those moments. I also sensed that my Dana, my guardian angel and my advocate, had been standing right there with me whispering in my ear, "Now just let it go, Mom."

During those days following the hearing, I sat with these competing emotions and was able to speak with my therapist, Rita, about my turmoil. All that I had experienced in that short exchange had opened my heart to accept that Patrick Ford was not just a monster with no sense of right and wrong, with no regret or sorrow for what he had done and taken from us. He was also a complicated, broken human being with feelings who now had to pay society for what he had done. Our judge had said that if Patrick Ford was in his self-imposed prison of guilt and remorse, it was something he would have to live with for the rest of his life, and that was worse than any sentence a judge could impose on him. Having heard his emotional statement to us, I believed he was, indeed, in his self-imposed prison. In the end, I had to follow my heart and my instincts and move on with the knowledge that I believed he was so sorry for what he had done.

I had learned so much about myself and my faith in those few days of reflection afterward. I was finally able to accept that I could trust my feelings and find some peace in all of them. I admitted to myself that I was okay with having forgiven him—not ever condoning what he had done, but forgiving him. How had I gotten to this place, this transformation of my heart?

This experience, up to that point in my journey, had been one of the most unequaled, profound events in my life. Even though I had never wavered from my belief that Dana had forgiven this young man, I still had not been able to do the same when I had walked into that hearing. But something miraculous had happened in the courtroom that day. All my prayers asking God for help to forgive Dana's murderer, something I felt was utterly impossible, had been answered when I heard Patrick Ford speak to us. That short exchange healed me in a way I had never expected or thought possible. How unbelievably powerful his heartfelt apology had been in helping me to forgive him. Reflecting, I have no doubt I had needed those two and a half years to heal and be open to hearing his words to us that day, as well as to be open to believing he was sincere. Not only had I gotten the closure I so desperately hoped for, but I had found peace with all that transpired on March 11, 2010. What I was not aware of was how much more there was to this story.

Two and a half years of my life had been focused on Dana's murder and its ramifications: coming to terms with the loss of my daughter, clawing my way out of the depths of grief and despair to find my path toward healing, choosing to participate in the lengthy court process, fighting to keep my marriage together, and during all that, remaining positive and not letting myself descend into darkness. Because I had still been grieving a life without my Dana, I had attempted to focus on moving forward in my emotional healing throughout the two years of court hearings. Yet subconsciously, a part of me had frequently been in a state of anxiety, frustration, and aggravation because of the grueling, drawn-out court process. It had become obvious in the days and weeks after the plea-agreement hearing that the whole experience had been emotionally and physically draining for me. I had to begin the process of decompressing myself from the heightened state of internal stress I had not even been aware of. My life had been on hold to some extent until we got an outcome. Intellectually, I knew we were free and that Patrick Ford was in prison, but I had to get to the place emotionally where I believed this was truly the end of the court process. When I was finally able to accept there would be no more worrying about missing an important hearing if we planned a vacation or any other special event, the final weight was lifted from me. I felt as free as a bird soaring in the sky. This decompression process took a few months until I gradually found myself more at peace than I had been in years. Now I could simply concentrate on living a full life.

CHAPTER 28

RETREATS

Within a few years after Dana's death, some of my close friends had begun to gently nudge and encourage me to write a book about my healing journey. They tried to convince me that my healing journey was inspirational and could help others. It took some years, but gradually I came to believe I did have something special to contribute. Finally, almost four and a half years after Dana's death, in early January 2012, I decided I was ready to tell my story. What had changed my mind?

Throughout the years since Dana had died, I had continued to contemplate why I had been left here and Dana had died. Was God's plan for me to find a calling where I could use my unique gifts to help others in some way, to do some good in this world? I still had not figured that out. And then in February 2011, St. James Catholic Church, my parish church, was offering a women's retreat weekend, CRHP (Christ Renews His Parish). When this retreat opportunity presented itself, I was intrigued. I did not sign up right away, however, as I tried to come up with any number of reasons why I could not attend. But some force kept drawing me back. I was getting better at recognizing when, just possibly, my God was nudging me and guiding me. So, I took a leap of faith and accepted the invitation. The CRHP retreat emphasizes continued growth (no matter where you are in your spiritual life) through prayer, inspiring presentations, and personal reflection. I went into this weekend with little or no expectations or knowledge of what would take place during the thirty-plus hours we would be together.

Right from the start, I recognized this spiritual experience was exactly what I needed for myself. I was astonished the Spirit had guided me to this weekend to replenish my spirit yet again. The retreat was so much more than I could ever have imagined—spiritual, emotional, reflective, thought provoking, personal, intimate, and fun. As the weekend progressed, I realized my own life story and faith journey had been extraordinary and that God had always been with me, even when I had not recognized His presence. When I left that weekend retreat I felt drained, but I was excited to see where the Spirit would take me next. Little did I realize yet what an incredible journey I had begun!

At this retreat, each participant had the choice to commit to a year of preparation and formation as well as facilitating the next retreat. I had an overwhelming desire to be a part of this process. I knew in my heart the Spirit had moved me to participate in that 2011 retreat, and now I had a once-in-a-lifetime opportunity to be open and see where the Spirit would take me. And so, in March 2011, I made the commitment to participate in our preparation and formation process to lead the 2012 CRHP retreat.

One of the most important tasks in preparation for leading the retreat was for our team to be led through a process of discernment about eight months before the retreat. Each of us has our own unique gifts to offer. In prayer, during the discernment evening, we were led into a time of silence, a time to allow our hearts and minds to be open, to allow the Spirit to guide us to understand what unique gift each of us would best offer to the retreat. In the end, I was humbled to have been guided and chosen to be a witness for the topic of reconciliation.

When I was chosen as the reconciliation witness at our discernment, I knew I must end my witness with the astounding spiritual awakening I had experienced from the plea-agreement hearing. How could I not include that? Patrick Ford had changed my healing path with his powerful words to us that day. I had hoped that in agreeing to be a reconciliation witness, I would find the words to share how the power of God had helped guide me to reconciliation many times. With faith, I had to trust the process that had succeeded for decades.

Reawakening

While composing my reconciliation witness, I realized I was eager to share the miracle of what had happened to me. What more powerful reconciliation story had there been in my entire life than forgiving the young man who had murdered my younger daughter! My life had been changed forever in that Spirit-guided encounter. When I completed my reconciliation witness, the result was the story of my unique faith journey—a story of the progression of my developing personal relationship with God, a deep relationship that had led me to repeatedly experience the healing powers of reconciliation. And I experienced firsthand that nothing is impossible for God! I *finally* understood without reservation that when I could forgive Patrick Ford, God's gift to me had been a return of lightness and peace to my soul. I felt such a huge burden lifted from me.

My participation in the 2011 retreat and then the preparation process for the 2012 retreat were indeed the final catalysts that influenced me to tell my story. That year of self-reflection and preparation, which had offered me such an extraordinary insight about my journey since Dana had died, only increased my strong desire to tell my story. If, in my complete brokenness, I had been able to climb out of the seemingly bottomless abyss from my deepest depths of despair to the peace and healing I had been gifted with, then I might succeed in making a difference by helping others in their unique healing journeys. And so, as 2012 began, just about a month before I would be a witness for the theme of reconciliation, I began writing my story.

As the days drew near for our retreat to begin, our team's anticipation and excitement were building. Our group had prayed for guidance that we would be able to give of ourselves emotionally and spiritually to this year's CRHP participants, in the hopes they might find some personal and spiritual enrichment in a safe and friendly environment. Just before I presented my reconciliation witness that weekend, I prayed some part of my story might resonate with even one woman and help her along her life's journey. Each witness had chosen a song to be played at the end of their presentation that touched them in some way. At the end of my witness, my chosen song, "Let the Healing Begin" by 4Him, was one that had deeply moved me to tears at last year's retreat. As the song played, each woman in the room could give me feedback or even just a hug. In those moments, my tears were flowing as I accepted their love, their compassion, and their honesty in the ways I had touched some of their lives. I have never experienced so profoundly the quote from Saint Francis of Assisi that says, "It is in giving that we receive." I believe I received so much more that day than I had given. I felt extremely blessed and grateful for that gift. In addition, I was humbled that in sharing my story, I had been able to help others.

My book-writing mission had intensified after sharing my reconciliation witness at that retreat. I was so emboldened after experiencing firsthand how sharing my life story and faith journey had affected the participants of our retreat. The fact I had touched their lives in some way reassured me that I might help others discover their own unique path through their pain and suffering. I looked forward to the challenge and believed this CRHP experience for me was the perfect way to end my book.

I should have known better . . .

The book writing continued as time permitted. Whenever I found some significant blocks of time outside my "regular-life" obligations and activities, I focused on my writing. At times, I was frustrated and aggravated because things were not happening in the time frame I had anticipated. This occurred often during the first year and a half or so while writing this book. I was so passionate about getting this story completed quickly. But as happens, life got in the way, and when that occurred, I always yearned to get back to my story.

What I eventually learned was that, each time I came back to writing after an extended break, I became aware that I had needed that respite for some clarification or new revelation. After several of these delays, it became quite clear to me that the Spirit had had a hand in directing my storytelling. I became convinced of this fact because of how I had originally planned to end my book. But as the years passed and I had still not finished, I discovered there was so much more to my story that needed to be told.

CHAPTER 29

A NEW STRUGGLE

In the years since the plea-agreement hearing, occasionally I thought of Patrick Ford, as well as his family. I never thought of him with hatred or revenge, but wondered how he was faring in prison. I prayed for him and I continue to do so. In addition, I wondered how his mother and his siblings were doing, and prayed for them as well. I believed then they were suffering the loss of their loved one in a different manner. On the other hand, I will never put them in the same place as any of us who knew and loved Dana, who have had to deal with and heal from the knowledge that our loved one was violently murdered. But as a mother, I can empathize with his mother. She has had to deal with and try to heal from the knowledge that her son took another life, and now he has to pay society's price by spending a long time in a state prison. As a mother, I believe that situation would break my heart in a completely different way, but would break it nevertheless.

Eventually that same pesky little voice that had spoken to me in the past crept into my consciousness, uninvited once again. However, this time I was in a different place in my healing journey. I had become more open to these sorts of questions or suggestions that seemed to come from nowhere. Now I had come to accept they were from the Spirit.

Would I ever want Patrick to read my book? Might I ever come to the place emotionally where I would want to write to Patrick or visit him in prison?

I had no qualms about Patrick reading this story if he chose to do so. However, I immediately discounted visiting him. I could not even begin to imagine ever doing so. The thought brought up feelings of anxiety and worry about what he was like now, and fear of the unknown. I had no connection with him except for the words he had spoken to us at the plea-agreement hearing almost three years earlier. On the other hand, I wondered if Patrick would ever write to me. It seemed likely I would not be the one to initiate any correspondence with him. But truthfully, I could not dismiss the idea of someday writing to him. I had no desire to do so at this time, but I could not deny feeling ambiguous about the possibility. Even though these questions were not something I thought about frequently, when they did enter my head, I pondered them and realized nothing yet had changed.

I do not recall when my sister, Tina, posed the question to me as to whether I had thought about sharing this book with Patrick, but I think it was sometime in early 2013. I did not hesitate in my reply: "Yes, I've thought about it, and I would have no problem having him read my story." My sister was not the only person who had wondered aloud whether I might be willing to share my story with him, but I do believe she was the catalyst for what has developed from that original conversation. After my response to Tina's question, a few months later she braved her next question. Had I ever imagined myself getting to the place where I would write to Patrick or visit him in prison?

What possessed her to even think it was okay to ask me such things? I realize her questions might seem shocking and insensitive to some. However, it may be easier to understand knowing that Tina and I had had some prior conversations regarding the plea-agreement process as well as my experience hearing Patrick's words to us that day. She and I had discussed how I had felt God's hand and Dana's intervention in that exchange. I had shared with her that I would never forget what he had done, but in forgiving, I had felt so much freer and lighter. I had been able to move forward with a great sense of peace. And we had talked about the fact that I continue, to this day, to strive to keep judgment out of the equation and leave the work of Patrick's salvation to God.

I am astounded when I think about how the Spirit was working in me, guiding me along a path without me realizing, often preparing me for what was to come by speaking to me in that silent little voice. Since I had already been nudged by the Spirit, my advocate, and had pondered those exact questions, I was not offended or shocked with Tina's latest inquiries. I shared with her that I was not yet ready to answer those questions. My priest friend and spiritual advisor, Father Joji, had suggested that whenever I was troubled or unsure of how to proceed, I should sit with the question, pray for guidance, and then wait. The answer would eventually become clear. Since this advice had worked before, I gladly left it up to the Spirit to guide me.

I was taken aback, though, for the bombshell Tina dropped on me one day in mid-2013. She shared her strong desire to write a letter to Patrick Ford telling him she and I had forgiven him, and that I was writing a book about my path to healing! In her faith journey, she had come to believe she was called to do this and hoped she would have my approval. I listened to all she had to say and then, without any hesitation, gave her my approval under one condition: I wanted to have her read that letter to me before mailing it to Patrick, because I needed to be reassured she had not misrepresented me in any way. She agreed. I realized I could not stop her from writing the letter, even if I did not approve. But I had no doubt I would strongly try to dissuade her from mailing the letter if she portrayed my experience and feelings incorrectly.

Luckily, we did not have to deal with that situation. When she had finished writing the letter to Patrick in November 2013, she read it to me over the phone. Although I had no desire to write my own letter then, I was amazed and deeply touched by Tina's compassionate words and her nonjudgmental attitude toward this young man. I gave her my blessing and prayed I could handle whatever transpired from this correspondence. And then the waiting began.

Would he reply to Tina's letter, and if so, how would he respond? Tina shared that she had written Patrick a letter with a few of our siblings as well as a few of her friends. Some of those people worried about how I was handling this situation. I certainly appreciated their love and concern for me. However, I felt I was taking care of myself in this matter. Tina also had relayed to me the several angry reactions she had received: how dare she take it upon herself to correspond with Patrick Ford, how insensitive and cruel she was for bringing this up to me and asking for my approval, what the hell was she thinking! Because of those reactions, I felt protective of Tina and did not wish her to be in the cross fire, no matter how this all turned out.

Tina called me when she received Patrick's first letter in February 2014 and asked if I would like to hear what he had written. Of course I would! Apparently, Patrick had attempted to write the letter numerous times without success. Then on his last attempt, he noticed the last line in Tina's letter to him, which stated, "I want you to know you were forgiven." After seven years of thinking about how to say he was sorry and how to beg for forgiveness, he had never thought about what to say afterward. All his focus in the earlier drafts had been on asking for forgiveness. Tina had given him that without reservation. He stated in his letter that she had done an amazing thing for him when he had only caused us pain. He was amazed by that and ended by thanking her for that gift, asking why she had forgiven him and how she had been able to do so.

Tina and I discussed our reactions to that first letter. Both of us were quite skeptical, afraid he might be telling Tina what he thought she would want to hear. Even though I had been able to forgive this young man several years earlier, doubt crept into my mind as to whether he was being truthful. My first impression was that his letter seemed honest and sincere, but maybe too good to be true. I wanted to believe what he said, but I could not trust him with just one letter.

Their correspondence continued with Tina responding to that first letter, asking him about the availability of mental health resources in prison as well as what prison conditions were like for him. His reply to her second letter arrived in March 2014. This letter touched me in that I believed he was genuinely sorry and wanted to make amends. As he had worked on getting healthy mentally, emotionally, and spiritually for the past seven years, he could not help but wonder about the devastation his actions had caused our family. At the very least, he desperately wanted to tell us how sorry he was. He ended his letter thanking her for caring about him and for offering this opportunity for healing. And it was in this letter that he asked Tina if she thought I would accept a letter from him.

That is when my inner struggle took on a life of its own. I had a strong suspicion when Tina sent her first letter to Patrick that Joe and Sarah would be angry. And they might be angry with me that I had not stopped her, as if I could have controlled that! At the time, I had made a conscious decision to keep this information to myself until I thought it necessary for them to know. I had had no idea what would come of her sending Patrick a letter and had wanted to wait to see what transpired. But now, as Tina and I talked about whether I wanted a letter from Patrick, I began to cry. She gently asked me if I was crying because I would feel disloyal to Dana by accepting a letter from him, to which I emphatically responded, "No!" I could not explain in the moment why I could not stop crying. I later realized it was more about me wanting to hear from Patrick but still not trusting that I could believe what he would say. Added to that was my fear of what Joe and Sarah would think of me. And now I would most likely be questioned as to how this information had come to me. I certainly did not want Joe and Sarah to be angry with Tina, but realized I would have no control over their reactions. For now, I recognized once again that I needed time to sit with this question. I sensed I would eventually agree to receive a letter from him. I knew, though, that my decision could not be rushed and that I needed some time to become comfortable with whatever I decided to do.

I had been a bit nervous about what might come of this correspondence between my sister and Patrick. I was somewhat paranoid about her letters possibly jeopardizing anything related to his sentence. I had no facts on which to base this fear, and although occasionally I had felt nervous about their corresponding, I did not request that she stop. I had learned repeatedly since Dana had died that, whenever I stop trying to control things that are not mine to control and I ask God to help me let go, life becomes so much more peaceful and simple. And so it happened that with each letter Tina received through early June 2014, I slowly learned more about this young man. I came to trust he was being honest and willing to open himself up to answer any questions. Thus, my paranoia gradually faded away.

Finally, in early June 2014, I gave Tina my answer. In the end, I was confident that I wanted a letter from Patrick, no matter what anyone else might think. I desperately wanted to hear what he had to say to my family and me. And I was confident that my God would take care of me no matter what the letter contained. What I was not sure about, though, was whether I would want to reply if I did indeed receive a letter. That was yet to be determined. Now I would have to figure out how to tell Joe and Sarah about how it happened that I might receive a letter from Dana's murderer!

When I finally got up the courage to do so, the conversation took on the exact tone I had feared, that both Sarah and Joe were furious about Tina writing a letter to Patrick. I was not at all surprised their anger would be directed at Tina. How dare she presume to think she had any right to correspond with him? She better not say anything about either of them in her letters to Patrick! I knew Tina had not mentioned them to date, and I would specifically inform her of their wishes going forward. I tried to focus on the important fact that her correspondence had led to him asking if I might accept a letter from him. With that in mind, I attempted to bring the conversation back to the fact that I wanted to get a letter from Patrick, no matter how this whole situation had come about. Eventually, their love for me shone brightly as they both agreed they wanted what was best for me in my healing journey. But they also both strongly expressed they were not interested in anything to do with Patrick Ford. I smile now as I think about a comment Sarah made as the conversation ended that night: "Well, it's not like you're going to be pen pals or anything like that!" I hesitated for a moment and then replied, "I don't know . . ." Knowing myself well, I could not reassure her that I would not write back to Patrick if I received a letter from him, and I was not going to lie to my daughter.

I had been faced with this new struggle that was not unexpected. When I had heard that little voice from the Spirit, I knew well enough that eventually I would need to do some meditating, praying, and waiting. Over and over throughout these past years since Dana's death, I had taken time to sort through all my conflicting emotions whenever I struggled with a decision about what was best for me in my emotional and spiritual health. And I had never once regretted any decision I made in moving forward in my life and in my healing. With anticipation and a little anxiety, I now looked forward to hearing from Patrick.

CHAPTER 30

DEVELOPING A SPIRITUAL CONNECTION

I received my first letter on July 23, 2014. Once again, little did I know what was in store for me along this path of my life's journey. I was brought to tears upon reading Patrick's words to me. The letter was relatively short, but his message was powerful.

Dear Mrs. Mangi,

As hard as this letter is for me to write I can only believe that it is that much harder for you to receive it. Thank you for allowing me to send this to you, it's something I've wanted to do for the past 7 years.

I think about you very often. I think about your daughter, Sarah, about your husband. And of course I always think about Dana. I think about how devastating this all must be and about how badly you all must hurt. I think about what I took from you. I think about how unfair this is for you. But mostly I pray. I pray that somehow each of you can find peace, that eventually the pain lessens. I pray every night for all of you because I so desperately want you all to be okay someday. I just hope those prayers are answered.

To tell you I'm sorry for what I've done would be an understatement. I've agonized over how to express my sorrow, regret and remorse for my actions. I've spent the last 7 years practicing my apology and to be perfectly honest I've never come close to anything that fits.

Barbara A. Mangi

There aren't words for how I feel. Even if I spent the rest of my life saying I'm sorry in every conceivable way it wouldn't be enough. So all I can do is to say I'm so sorry and I promise I will spend the rest of my life trying to be the best person I can be. It won't be enough but I want to try to give back to the world what I took when I took Dana's life. I don't believe I'll ever be able to give to the world what she did and would have continued to do but I'll try with everything I am.

I don't know if you'll write back but, if you do, I'd really like to know how you and your family are doing. As you know, I've been corresponding with Tina. She let me know about your book & a little bit of how you've healed. Knowing that has helped me so much.

Talking to Tina has been incredible for me. You truly have an amazing sister. In my last letter to her I asked specifically about your husband and Sarah. I always wonder how they are doing. Are they okay? I remember Sarah's statement from court and I could feel her pain through her words. Your husband wasn't there but you talked about his pain. Their pain tore through me and I just want so badly for them to be okay.

There is something personal I'd like to ask you . . . I asked Tina the same question: How? How can you forgive me after what I've done? I'm hoping that, if I can understand how you did it, maybe I can learn to forgive myself.

I wish there was more for me to say. Some other ways to say sorry, to offer prayers. In the end, I can only thank you for letting me write this.

I hope that you're okay. And please know that if there is ever anything I can do to help you or your family all you have to do is ask. All that I am or ever will be is dedicated to your daughter.

Take care and God bless.

Sincerely,
Patrick Ford

Reawakening

As soon as I received Patrick's letter, even though they had expressed no interest in any correspondence from him, I asked both Sarah and Joe whether they wanted to read the letter. Each of them declined and stated that if I did respond to his letter, they did not want me to share anything about them. In a conversation with Sarah within a week or so after that first conversation, she asked me to read the letter to her. After hearing his letter, she said that if I decided to reply to Patrick, I could share with him that she had found peace in her life, but nothing else. And so, I would respect their wishes.

My decision was easy; there was no doubt in my mind I would answer this letter. Never once did I feel any guilt or sense that somehow I was betraying my Dana. Since I had taken the time to meditate and pray about corresponding with Patrick, I was confident this was the right decision for me. Patrick's most pressing questions were how I had been able to forgive him, followed by how my family and I were doing. Just as with my book writing, some of his most profound questions required much reflection, meditation, prayer, and careful consideration. As I wrote my response, I expressed that I would be honest in answering his questions so he could understand where I came from and where I had progressed in my healing process, even if some of what I said might be painful to hear. My goal was certainly not to hurt him with my words, but to try to convey that he had played an important part in eventually helping me forgive him. As honestly and compassionately as I could, I answered Patrick's first letter and our correspondence began. It took me about two months to compose this first letter. At the time, I had not shared with either Sarah or Joe that I had written back to Patrick, and neither of them asked me about it.

In that letter, I concentrated on explaining my road to forgiving him. I did not mince words as I tried to describe what I had thought of him up until the plea-agreement hearing, all that I had done to help myself heal, and my failure to forgive him before hearing him speak to us on March 11, 2010. I concluded with my belief that he too had been on a healing journey those past seven years, and with my hope that he might forgive himself.

Barbara A. Mangi

Dear Patrick,
September 17, 2014

First of all, thank you for writing to me. For quite a few years now, I had wondered if I would ever hear from you. I guess I hoped that I would, but was also scared that I would receive a letter from you. I can only imagine the amount of courage and strength it took for you to come to your decision to write to me. For that I am grateful.

You asked me about how I was able to forgive you. I have struggled these weeks as to how I could answer your very complicated and profound question. It is extremely hard to put into words how I got to the place where I could forgive you, but I'll try my best to explain. In the end, I hope that my honesty will help you to understand where I came from and where I am now in my healing process, even if some of what I say is painful to hear. My goal is certainly not to hurt you with my words, but to try to convey to you that you played an important part in eventually helping me to forgive you.

I believe it starts with my faith journey. In writing my book, I discovered much about myself in relationship to my God. I have come to realize that I've had a pretty strong faith since I was quite young. I can only surmise that something I was taught in Catholic grade school instilled in me my belief in the existence of a loving and kind God.

My road to forgiving you, Patrick, has been a long journey. I had no idea early on how to save myself from drowning in my overwhelming grief and my longing to have my Dana back. Honestly, it was a struggle for me to get through every minute of every day for some time. But something kept me going. Unquestionably, my faith is what gave me some hope, peace, comfort, and consolation. And, although I was near emotional collapse, I never gave up on this God of mine or blamed God for what had happened to Dana, as some people do. My God has always been a loving God, not a vengeful or punishing God, and so my most personal relationship with God began to deepen as I prayed.

Without a doubt, one of the most significant spiritual experiences in my life to date was my journey from just trying to survive Dana's death to a return to the lightness and peace I feel today. I don't really remember much about those first several weeks after our lives were changed forever. But I do know that I was struggling to make sense of what had happened and why, as well as beginning to subconsciously redefine what my new normal would be without Dana. Eventually I began questioning how I would be able to survive this tragedy and if I could ever be happy again. Even in my broken emotional state though, without conscious thought, I had begun to slowly define what I needed to heal, right from the very beginning, and I continued that process daily.

I found several resources early on to help me find any fleeting moment of peace from the turmoil within me. Listening to beautiful, inspirational, soothing music, reading books dealing with grief and books of daily reflections, meeting with a psychologist, journaling without any regard to editing, spending time with women friends who could share in my grief openly, and finding ways to keep Dana's memory alive—all of these things brought me solace and comfort at times.

There was one additional thing I had always taken comfort in, no matter what challenging situations I faced throughout my life, and that was prayer. And now I prayed in sorrow, in confusion, in questioning, in thanksgiving, in anguish. In this ancient act of praying, I knew I would find refuge, peace, and consolation. My God would be with me, taking care of me no matter what happened, of that much I was confident.

Isaiah 43:2
When you pass through waters, I will be with you; through rivers, you shall not be swept away.

When you walk through fire, you shall not be burned, nor will flames consume you.

My path towards healing was filled with quite a few roadblocks along the way, some that were out of my control and others over which I had some control. I do know that from pretty early on it was inconceivable to me, at this point in my very tenuous healing journey, that I could ever get to a place where I could forgive you, Patrick. It seemed impossible. However, on the other hand, I want you to know that I never thought of you with hatred or revenge in my heart. Back then, though, I sadly thought of you as "a psycho monster" who might be pretending to be insane in order to avoid going to prison. I could not comprehend why you did this, so I did not want you back out on the street. I simply wanted justice, to have you pay your debt to society as the consequences for what you had done. My overriding emotion was fear of you hurting my beautiful Sarah or any other innocent young woman if you were released from jail.

The passing of time, my strong faith, the love and support of my entire family and my amazing friends, and the choices I made along the way that helped me begin to heal, all finally led me to see a light in the distance. I consciously chose to move away from the darkness of despair and agony over losing my Dana and instead chose to move towards the light of seeing her life as a gift from God. I chose to avoid the darkness of hate-filled and revengeful thoughts towards you. And I chose to do whatever I could to move towards the light, to do whatever I needed to do for me that would help me eventually heal.

Even as I slowly started to heal I continued to struggle, wondering if I could ever truly forgive, not to condone or really ever forget what you did, but to forgive you. I knew in my heart, of course, that is what our God asks of us. I had learned that the power of God's message is that when I forgive others, I am forgiven.

But how could He ask me to do that for someone who murdered my Dana?

For the next two years or so, I continued to pray for God to help me forgive, even though I didn't know how He could accomplish that in me. At times, I cried because of this huge weight I felt on me.

Psalm 13:3
How long must I carry sorrow in my soul,
grief in my heart day after day?

At the plea agreement on March 11, 2010, I was totally convinced that you did not care and would not show any sorrow or remorse when I read my impact statement. But I was so wrong! One of the totally unexpected moments for me was when you asked the judge if you could address the Mangi family. I could see you VERY clearly for the first time because you were so close to me, and I heard you loud and clear. I saw the pain in your eyes and heard the quivering in your voice as with strong emotion you spoke to us, looking Sarah and me straight in the eye. As I listened to you, your apology brought up a sense of compassion in me and, shockingly, a feeling of sadness for you—for what your life would be because of what you did. I struggled with knowing I felt that way that day. I felt traitorously guilty for these feelings, thinking how I could feel that way for the person who killed my precious daughter. But, in those few moments as you addressed us, I realized that you were not just a monster with no regret or sorrow for what you had done and what you had taken from us, but a complicated, broken human being with feelings who now had to pay society for what he did.

Because you chose to address us that day and because you acknowledged what you had done to Dana and to all of us who love her, that very short exchange healed me in a way I never expected or thought possible. From the beginning, I never doubted that Dana would have forgiven you, Patrick.

I had struggled and prayed to God for help in doing the same. I didn't know how I could ever get to that place. Thinking back on my healing journey, I believe wholeheartedly that God had gently nudged and guided me through those years to lead me to the place where I was able to be open to all you said that day and to absorb your heartfelt message to us. Astoundingly, God answered all of my prayers and I felt such a huge burden lifted from me. That profound moment changed my life. With that, I was able to forgive you and begin to move forward with a sense of peace.

> *Psalm 23:1–4, 6*
> *The LORD is my shepherd;*
> *there is nothing I lack.*
> *In green pastures he makes me lie down;*
> *to still waters he leads me;*
> *he restores my soul.*
> *He guides me along right paths*
> *for the sake of his name.*
> *Even though I walk through the valley of the shadow of death,*
> *I will fear no evil, for you are with me;*
> *your rod and your staff comfort me.*
>
> *Indeed, goodness and mercy will pursue me*
> *all the days of my life;*
> *I will dwell in the house of the LORD*
> *for endless days.*

Everyone in the courtroom with me that day was on their own individual journey of grief and healing and each would have heard and interpreted your words based on their own unique circumstances. I can only speak for myself in how I felt and absorbed your message. I don't know and will never know if I would have ever been able to forgive you if you had not addressed us that day. All I know for sure is that my life changed in a miraculous way.

I felt Dana's intervention and God's hand at work in that exchange on March 11, 2010.

I truly believe you, too, have been on your own unique spiritual journey since Dana died. Through your letters to Tina, I know that you are continually working on your spiritual healing. It seems to me that the loving and compassionate God that I believe in has been near to you, has had a "hand in your life" in prison, has brought you into the light to some extent, and has guided you to trust in His plan for you now. It seems as if God has been working through both you and me these last 7 years. He brought each of us to the place we needed to be—for you to be able to speak to us from your pain and sorrow for what you had taken from us and for me to be able to accept that what you were saying was truly from your heart—to bring about that miraculous reconciliation that began to heal us both.

> *Psalm 30:3, 12–13*
> *O LORD, my God,*
> *I cried out to you for help and you healed me.*
> *You changed my mourning into dancing;*
> *you took off my sackcloth*
> *and clothed me with gladness.*
> *So that my glory may praise you*
> *and not be silent.*
> *O LORD, my God,*
> *forever will I give you thanks.*

I cannot say I will ever forget what you did, but in forgiving your actions, I feel so much freer and lighter. I want you to know, Patrick, I don't dwell on how Dana died, but always try to keep all of my treasured memories of her close to my heart. I have been attending a support group since early in 2008 called POMC, Parents of Murdered Children, and am the only member of our current group who has ever had the perpetrator of their loved one's murder take responsibility for what they had done. And all of my friends in this group see how much I have healed from having heard your apology that day.

My heart breaks for each of them and, at the same time, makes me feel incredibly blessed that I was in a place to hear and to accept your apology. My prayer for each of them is always that somehow they will be able to get to a place of peace and lightness too.

Patrick, I hope you have seen how powerful your words were in helping me to heal, in helping me to come to a place where I was able to forgive you, and in contributing to where I am today. I believe that you are already a very spiritual person, based on what you have shared in your letters to Tina. I pray that, continuing on your own journey of healing, reconciliation, and redemption, you will find a way to forgive yourself.

Psalm 34:19
The LORD is close to the brokenhearted,
saves those whose spirit is crushed.

My husband, Joe, WAS in court that day and heard your apology. Sarah has found peace in her life and Joe does not want me to share anything about him. I will respect that wish.

I have enclosed the prayer card from Dana's funeral for you and also the lyrics to one of my most inspirational songs that may be helpful to you in your search for forgiveness. If I can help you in any way to continue on your healing journey, you can write back to me.

In forgiveness and peace,
Barb Mangi

Patrick was, more often than not, much quicker to respond than I was. In the beginning of our letter writing, we had both promised to be honest in responding to each other's questions. With that promise, for me, there slowly arose a mutual respect and I began to trust the budding connection that was developing. Eventually, through our corresponding, Patrick and I developed a deep emotional connection and a spiritual bond. And with every one of his letters, I learned more and more about this young man and how he was handling prison life as well as continuing his road to emotional, mental, and spiritual healing.

Throughout these last two years, we have developed what I call a spiritual connection that is miraculous in and of itself, we have come to share an unusually unique relationship with each other, and we have discovered that some of our life experiences mirrored each other.

Excerpts from Patrick's letter to Barb: October 2014

> *Thank you. Thank you for everything your letter gave to me. I finally felt that lightening of the spirit that others have described. I don't know if this is a permanent feeling or just momentary grace but at least for now I feel peace. Like you, I have always felt a close connection to God. Unlike you, I did respond with a sense of anger and betrayal towards God. Over the past 7 years I've worked to repair that relationship with God and today after reading your letter I feel his presence more fully than I ever have. Thank you.*
>
> *... Of course, if there is anything you want to know from/about me or just anything you need to say please, please feel free. This may seem like a strange thing to say but as far as I am concerned my life is completely open to you and your family. In a perfect world all of our relationships could be filled with love and grace. However, I'm completely blessed to simply have your forgiveness.*
>
> *Your letter was very open and honest. I'll never truly understand what you felt but you allowed me a clear glimpse.*

Your candidness meant so much to me. I hope and pray that every day brings further healing. Thank you so much for the prayer card. It feels good to have it. It brings love and peace. Thank you again & again for everything. I truly believe God has worked through you and your sister to help heal my heart . . . I don't know if you'd be open to the idea but I would very much like to hear from you. I'm interested in how you are today, how you've coped and what you went through.

Excerpts from Patrick's letter to Barb: December 2014

I was very happy to receive another letter from you & more than a little relieved. I still worry about saying the wrong thing & causing additional pain. So my letters go out with a fair amount of trepidation. I'm just glad to hear that my letters don't hurt you. From your letter it sounds like you have similar concerns. For what it's worth, you don't have to worry about what you write to me. I'm so incredibly amazed by the kindness and compassion that you (and Tina) have shown me that I take everything you say with the belief that it is aimed at healing. I'm also very aware that healing can at times be painful and I accept that fully.

My healing journey is a miracle to me. I didn't believe I'd ever get over the pain and sorrow I felt for taking Dana's life. I truly believed healing was an impossibility for me. Even as the years progressed and I slowly healed & regained stability there was still this gaping hole. I thought this hole was permanent. My relationship with you and Tina has rapidly been healing that wound and closing that hole. I don't think I was ever really willing to heal without your permission. Maybe I just needed to hear you say it was okay for me to get better, to let the pain go. I used to feel this acute pain whenever I imagined getting better before you. It seemed so unfair for me to be okay if you weren't. I don't know how logical this thought was but I took it seriously and never allowed myself to fully heal. Hearing from you and receiving a measure of your compassion literally opened the floodgates of God's grace. I can't thank you enough for this . . .

Excerpts from Barb's letter to Patrick: January 2015

. . . I read your letter quickly the day I received it because I was very busy. That evening I attended a beautiful and unique prayer service called Taizé . . . From my very first experience [in January 2010], I found that Taizé prayer calmed and quieted my soul, allowing me to find inner silence so that my God could touch my heart . . . This type of meditative prayer drew me in that very first night and I have come to love this reflective, quiet time of peaceful prayer and beautiful chants.

. . . During our meditative time of silence, I was completely overcome with so many thoughts and emotions because your letter had touched me to the core on so many levels. I didn't know it, but I needed to be there that evening to take the time to let my God help me sort through all I was feeling.

Many things were going through my head during that time of rich silence, all jumbled up but powerful nonetheless . . . I'll try to explain . . .

I marveled at the connection we have at this time and at this place in each of our lives, even after all that had transpired.

I was in awe that we both feel that our healing journeys have been a miracle, and even more amazing, that we started from completely opposite places to come together in this most astounding, life-giving miracle of all. My words are so inadequate to describe how this affects me when I take the time to truly reflect on how God has brought us together . . .

It brought tears to my eyes thinking that it was my sister who was the catalyst for all that has happened among the three of us since she sent her first letter. From reading your first five letters to her, I learned so much more about you as *a person, as a broken human being. Because you willingly opened yourself to us, shared with us your pain and sorrow for what you had done, I came to trust that you were being honest with us. This finally gave me the courage to agree to letting you write to me. Tina, however, had the courage and the heart to take the risk of initiating a correspondence with you without knowing what to expect. Her beautiful spirit and light from within shines brightly.*

... I have wondered for years what my purpose might be in this world, what God had been preparing me to do ... Just maybe, all I've been through in my life, all of my personal struggles, my losses and heartaches, my joys and blessings, had prepared me to connect with you, Patrick, to let you know how I had been able to forgive you and that I prayed for your continued healing. In wonderment and awe, as my tears were flowing for what God can accomplish through us, eventually I acknowledged that, just possibly, this is where my God has meant for me to be at this time in my life. I could hardly take all of these thoughts in and process that God chose me to help you to heal and begin to forgive yourself. Never could I have imagined this scenario in the early years following Dana's murder. But, humbly, here I am and I am at peace.

Excerpt from Patrick's letter to Barb: February 2015

... I was inspired by your letter and moved, quite literally, beyond words. Your level of trust in God and your capacity for forgiveness has [sic] *left me slightly dumbfounded. I haven't been able to find the words to express how positively your letter affected me.*

... I want to thank you for your courage. You commented that you've struggled with how others might view you for writing to me. I hadn't thought of that before. When I did, the immensity of it came crashing into my awareness. I had

assumed that there might be people who questioned, "How could you write to your daughter's murderer?" But I always assumed that question would be laced with admiration. To think that there might be those who didn't understand or disagreed with your writing me changed how I view this. I already was beyond grateful, and in awe of your forgiveness. But now I respect your courage on a new level.

... I'm humbled by all of this. For the briefest moments I glimpse how big God is and how truly powerful He is and I'm brought to my knees. Then I'll experience His love and I'll lose all forms of expressing how I feel. Words just don't work. It's too much to describe. I hear your words and I can feel the Holy Spirit moving through and guiding them. How then do I respond to that? Honestly I never feel up to the task. Your words echo my feelings and I get stuck ...

Excerpt from Barb's letter to Patrick: May 2015

... Thank you for your compliments on my being courageous about writing to you. But I actually feel like quite a coward because I just cannot bring myself to open up to my family and friends about this relationship of ours. I am not one who wants to be the center of attention and I know that I do not want any attention drawn to me because of our amazing story. I cannot imagine being able to clearly explain a miracle in a concise and compassionate manner. And, yet, I also feel like I am now fighting against God's calling for me to announce how He lovingly and miraculously works through us, His very imperfect children!

Excerpt from Patrick's letter to Barb: May 2015

... Sometimes I want to write to you just to ask how you're doing. I have this urge to write just to let you know you're on my mind. Several times I've started letters where I just ask, "how are you?" and then I realize I have nothing else to write. I'm still so unsure of the nature of our new relationship. I can't imagine it's any easier for you. Yet as unsure and hesitant as I sometimes feel, at the same time I'm eager to write to you and to hear back. It is unique to say the least. So I guess for this letter I'll just ask. How are you? How is your family? I know your husband doesn't want to be included in these letters but I hope he is well.

It can be difficult for me at times to wonder about and care so much for people and yet have no tangible way to express that concern. Maybe that's what this letter will do.

As for myself, I'm doing remarkably well. Especially since Tina and yourself [sic] began writing to me. Letting go of my guilt was both infinitely harder and easier than I could have imagined. On my own it was impossible but with a few words of forgiveness it melted away. Since then I've been discovering a peace that I've been searching for my whole life. It is still a bit fleeting because I will at times get caught up in the mundane. But more and more I find myself in that center of peace and love. I've been sharing parts of our journey with fellow inmates in the hope that they can experience this peace as well.

Excerpt from Barb's letter to Patrick: June 2015

...Ours is an unusually unique relationship to say the least. It's hard to imagine, much less be in it with you. So I have just decided to let go and put this, too, in the hands of the Spirit to guide me. I do have times when I think of you, hoping you are okay and still moving ahead in your healing journey. I find that I am a bit lighter when I hear that more and more you find yourself in that center of peace and love that you have been searching for your whole life...

I am doing well, Patrick. I really, truly am. Emotionally and mentally, I am more at peace than I've been in many *years. I had so much emotional baggage from childhood that it took decades to begin to heal from those scars. But I was in a relatively good place in 2007 before the bottom dropped out. Dana's death almost crushed me and did break my heart and my spirit, yet, it was also the catalyst for me to find a path to the light and peace that had eluded me in some relationships. I, too, had to be totally broken, in a different way than you were, but broken nevertheless, to be able to give myself totally up to my God because I could not find the way on my own. I fought with all I had in me to come back to the light, to find joy, happiness, contentment, and peace in my soul. I know it's so difficult for people to believe that, but it is the truth.*

The difficult part about sharing my life today with you is that my life isn't in a vacuum. It also includes my husband and my daughter. And, since I have to respect their wishes about not sharing anything about them with you, it is hard to write a letter that excludes them in my life's journey. What I will share is that they are each on their own journey, each different than mine and different from each other. I am at peace where they each are on their journey and I believe they are doing well, considering the circumstances . . .

Excerpts from Patrick's letter to Barb: July 2015

. . . Like you, hearing that you are doing well brings me incredible measures of peace. For some reason I was a little more nervous than usual regarding this past letter. I'm not really sure what prompted the increased nervousness but your response really put me at ease. Your decision to let go and put the process in the hands of the Spirit inspired me to do the same . . .

Our relationship is definitely, as you put it, "unusually unique." That scares me at times. Maybe nervous or hesitant would be better words than scared. Regardless, getting out of the way and letting go is a constant effort when writing letters to you. Yet at the same time it is one of my favorite things to do.

. . . You made a comment in your letter that was very powerful and really spoke to me. "I too, had to be totally broken, in a different way than you were but broken nevertheless, to be able to give myself totally up to my God because I could not find the way on my own." That line stunned me. It inspired one of those moments where I was able to see the interconnectedness of us all. Those words echoed my thoughts so completely that for a moment there was no difference. Two people couldn't be farther apart in a situation yet the interior aspects could still mirror each other. I felt the presence of the Divine in your words. When you commented that it's difficult to convince people of this truth, I felt completely understood. I can never convince people that being broken down fully was the only way for me to be rebuilt. Your experience being so similar was amazing to me . . .

Excerpt from Barb's letter to Patrick: December 2015

I am in awe of how opening myself to reach out to you, Patrick, and letting you into my life, has changed and enriched my life. I put aside my fears, doubts, and many uncertainties about my decision and put all of that in God's hand to take care of me. And, in doing so, I can truly agree that what God wants for me and from me is NOT what I could have ever expected in my lifetime . . .

Excerpts from Patrick's letter to Barb: January 2016

I was very happy to receive your letter. Granted I'm always happy to hear from you. I was a little worried because it had been a while. I started to let my mind wander and began thinking up scenarios in which I offended you with my last letter. I managed to think myself into circles and tied myself up emotionally. Then the most wonderful thing happened. I stopped trying to control things and just trusted that God's will was being done. I felt the tension melt away and was incredibly grateful for that lesson. It's a lesson I've had to learn time and time again, yet each time I am happy that I have the opportunity to keep trying. Of course, as is typically the case, right after I let go of my anxiety I received your letter. I thought that would be a fun story to share.

Speaking of sharing, I'm in a class called "Houses of Healing." In the class we read a book by the same name and discuss how we can relate to the lessons. Fairly soon we'll be covering the chapter on Restorative Justice . . . briefly it is a focus on restoring the broken relationships caused by criminal offenses rather than focusing solely on punishment. One of the key elements of restorative justice is the victim/offender reconciliation. Basically it's an opportunity for the victim or the victim's family to confront the offender. To explain how they were hurt and how their lives have changed. Sometimes it's just a forum for the families to vent. Oftentimes offenders are able to answer questions and help facilitate mutual healing. This, of course, is exactly what we have been doing through our letters. When we reach the chapter in our class I plan on speaking and sharing my own experience. I've mentioned this to Tina and she has encouraged me to share our journey. With your permission I'd like to share our story as well. I think your gift of forgiveness will be a powerful example for other inmates. If you aren't comfortable with this I will speak only in vague terms . . .

Please if you feel at all uneasy about me sharing let me know & I won't . . .

Barbara A. Mangi

Excerpts from Barb's letter to Patrick: February 2016

... Patrick, I am surprised and happy that you are able to attend a class about victim/offender reconciliation ... It's unbelievable that our situation is actually a successful example for advocating for restorative justice and the VORP [Victim/Offender Reconciliation Program]. We have seen how powerfully it can change lives as obviously it has worked for you and me, at least. I do strongly believe that focusing on the possibility of restoring broken relationships and having opportunities for inmates to begin to heal is so much healthier than simply focusing on punishment. Sounds like a wonderful program for those offenders wishing for some chance at reconciliation.

I would like to say that I am totally comfortable right now with you sharing our story ... but something is holding me back. I know myself well enough now to know that I need some time to process all of this. Since time is of the essence for you, if I change my mind in the near future, I'll send you a quick note to that affect [sic]. In any case, Patrick, I would love to get your feedback when you do share your story.

Thank you for understanding that I might not be comfortable yet and for honoring my wishes.

Excerpts from Patrick's letter to Barb: April 2016

... You had asked some questions about my class. The class isn't specifically about victim/offender reconciliation but rather about healing ourselves and all of our relationships. Victim/offender reconciliation is just one aspect of the class. We have been able to read about and discuss successful stories from other states ...

Much of the rest of the class is a forum for inmates to share their stories and to discuss the bad choices and negative consequences of their lives. Also it allows for guys to really explore the circumstances and ultimately the "why" they made the choices they did . . . What's so very interesting to me is to see who these men are now especially compared to the stories of who they used to be. In almost every case the person of the past no longer exists and a new stronger, healthier person has taken their place.

The state doesn't officially support the program but they allow for volunteers to come in and conduct classes. For our class, Lori (a Lutheran minister), teaches the class. She's been coming to Stateville for over twenty years. Her focus is on rehabilitation rather than punishment. Her view is that many (well maybe not many but some) of the inmates will go home some day and it is important to help bring back a productive member of society. And as for the "lifers" or men with so much time as to make no difference, at least they can find some peace. Really she is a remarkable person. At no point do any of us deny the justice in our incarceration but we try to become more than just our crimes and to do our best to move on.

. . . So I wanted to spend some time in this letter to thank you for being so open and candid with me. I can't imagine what you experience in relation to my questions and your answers.

Knowing that you're healing helps me heal. But also knowing the hurt you felt & still experience helps as well. Early on I think I may have been looking to punish myself by trying to feel your pain. It gave me more ammunition against myself. However, as I've forgiven myself I find that your hurt keeps me reminded of how important it is that I keep working. Knowing the real life consequences of my actions only motivates me more to be better. An abstract idea of consequences can certainly help fuel growth but the deeper understanding just matters more. I hope that makes sense. I guess it's just another of the ways that you help me. Your story doesn't hurt me the way it did (a little still) but rather guides me on a very deep emotional and spiritual level. Thank you for that.

... I appreciate so much your willingness to share with me. You mentioned in regards [sic] to your book that you have doubts about ever adequately explaining how your life has changed. I feel that way whenever I read one of your letters and try to respond. I feel so insufficient to the task that it's borderline laughable. The immensity of all this is sometimes startling and all I want to do is just talk about how incredible it has been. So thank you. No matter how often or in how many different ways I attempt to say it, it isn't enough. How great is God? I can only be in awe of His work.

Excerpts from Barb's letter to Patrick: May 2016

You said in your letter that knowing I'm healing helps you to heal ... You followed this by stating, "Knowing the real life consequences of my actions only motivates me more to be better. An abstract idea of consequences can certainly help fuel growth but the deeper understanding just matters more."

Those words, Patrick, were very enlightening to me as, once again, amazingly I see a mirror image of our experiences. Let me try to explain ...

In reading your words, it got me to thinking about why our relationship has been helping me to heal even more profoundly than I ever thought I needed. Early on, for me, I sadly thought of you as just Dana's murderer. I couldn't imagine much else about you as a person, Patrick, until you spoke at the plea agreement hearing. That was the catalyst for opening my heart to accept that you were more than the crime you committed. And, then, the floodgates opened when I began to read your letters to Tina. Finally, when I agreed to let you write to me, I personally began to get a much deeper understanding of the kind of young man you are.

So, when I only knew you abstractly, I could not see you as anything more than your crime. But when I heard your words to us that day at the plea agreement hearing and then, with each additional choice I made to let myself be open to your words in the letters to Tina and then to me, I came to believe that you are much more than your crime. Once I had a much deeper and personal understanding of your life's journey, I was able to see you as a multifaceted, complicated, spiritual, caring young man.

. . . I am truly astounded as I think about how the Holy Spirit was working in me, guiding me along a path without me realizing it, and always lovingly and gently preparing me for what was to come. Patrick, I'm guessing that you probably feel the same way with God working within you. Our experiences continue to mirror each other. I couldn't have said it better myself when you said "The immensity of all this is sometimes startling and all I want to do is just talk about how incredible it has been . . . How great is God? I can only be in awe of His work."

Excerpt from Patrick's letter to Barb: July 2016

Thank you for your last letter. Not only did you answer all of my questions but you also gave me great insight into your journey. I tend to worry alot [sic] about how my thoughts, words and actions affect people. I don't want to be the cause of any trouble or pain. With you that feeling is even stronger . . . I still see our relationship as very delicate and fragile. Maybe this is just a projection on my part because of how important this is to me. It could be fear of losing something so necessary. Regardless of the reason for my worry, it was reassuring to hear your response.

. . . Most everything told about prison is bad and rightly so. But there is good even here. Many of the best people I've met are guys serving life sentences. At times it is impossible

to process that the person I'm talking to is the same person that committed murder or some other horrible crime. Maybe I'm not. Maybe they are no longer the same person. The people they've become are wonderful, kind, loving human beings. Knowing them has made me better. They are living examples of the change that is possible.

. . . Prison isn't anything like I expected. In a lot of ways it's worse but I'm still surprised to meet so many good and decent people. Certainly not all but far more than I expected. For example, the guys in my class are all willing to take honest looks at themselves and to try and change. It's encouraging.

. . . I was finally able to do my presentation [for Houses of Healing class]. *It went really well . . . I just talked. I told them of the journey of healing and forgiveness. About how freeing it was to apologize and express my remorse. Basically about how transformative it has been. Of course I started with the first letter from Tina and how I was terrified to read it. And how it was even more frightening to reply . . . I told them about our letters* [letters between Tina and Patrick] *and how they brought healing and love to both of us. I mentioned that you and I write but didn't get into details. But I told them how great it's been. The response from the class was awesome. The most common emotion was regret . . . For the most part the guys in the class saw in our relationship the final piece of healing they were searching for. Sadly they have to make a choice between that peace and their legal case.* [So many of them were still filing appeals, and any contact between them and the victim's family is against the law.] *I can't make that choice for them but I know how unhappy and broken I was even before prison. What is the point of freedom if you're locked in a prison of your own mind and heart? I suppose each person's journey is their own . . .*

I've been thinking a lot about our experiences mirroring each other. Then you said our divine journeys have collided. I like that way of viewing it more . . . I think of you as my partner on this journey. Without you I just don't think it would have been possible for me. At the very least we are following the same guide. I'm grateful for this. Sometimes I wonder where this goes but I try not to get ahead of myself. I trust God and His plan. Considering where I was and where I am now how can I not trust?

When responding to Patrick's first letter to me back in September 2014, I was not ready to share this budding correspondence with anyone, except for just a few girlfriends, because of those earlier reactions I had heard from Tina. I did not even tell Joe or Sarah I was responding to his letters, because they wanted nothing to do with him. As time passed, I would not have hesitated sharing my experience with them if either had asked if Patrick and I were corresponding. But if they did not ask, I was not going to bring it up until I was ready to do so. And so it went during that first year of our correspondence. Then, in September 2015, while Sarah and I were on a hiking trip in Spain, she finally raised the question about whether Patrick and I were writing to each other. It was then that I could explain what had transpired and how Patrick and I had developed what I would call a spiritual connection. I had no idea how Sarah would respond in hearing that not only were Patrick and I writing to each other regularly but that we had developed this type of friendship. As Sarah and I hiked in the beautiful countryside of Spain, there were no distractions and we had as much time as we needed to complete our discussion. My self-imposed burden, that of keeping this huge piece of myself from all those who know me and love me, was lightened tremendously when Sarah accepted where I was in my heart and my soul in regard to Patrick and our spiritual connection. But this experience with Sarah reaffirmed my belief that I needed those types of one-on-one opportunities, with no time constraints or distractions, for my storytelling.

As these years have passed, I have longed to share this miraculous experience with those I love most: Joe, our families, and some of my closest friends. I had already come to the place where I felt like only a few people knew the real me now, and it saddened me. But I was overwhelmed believing I would never be able to explain in just a short conversation all that has transpired and how I came to this place. Regrettably, the few times I thought I would have the opportunity for a deeper conversation, the situation never presented itself. So instead, I stuck with my decision and thought that eventually I would know the right time to share that Patrick Ford and I had been corresponding for a while.

CHAPTER 31

MY PERSONAL AND UNIQUE RELATIONSHIP WITH GOD

One afternoon, sometime in mid-2015, I was struggling to explain to Father Joji how I could describe the connection that had developed between Patrick and me to anyone, much less to myself. His insightful and powerful words that day helped me put everything into perspective: "Barb, you are on a divine journey with Patrick Ford." This profound yet simple statement touched me to the depth of my being. When I later took time to reflect on our conversation that day, I felt as if I had been struck by a bolt of lightning as I acknowledged in wonder, in thanksgiving, and in joy how truly deep and enduring was my personal relationship with God. And in that trusting relationship that had developed with this God I had put my faith in, I had been guided on this unbelievable journey with Patrick Ford.

Never had I imagined what a personal relationship with God would entail. To develop, it requires spending time together, respectfully listening to and talking to each other, meditating and praying, trusting in the relationship, learning to live, and trying to follow the golden rule: "Do to others whatever you would have them do to you." At times throughout my life I had questioned my God, I had been angry with God, I had taken advantage of God's goodness by not spending the time required to stay in a close, personal relationship. But my God can handle all of this because He has unconditional love for us. Yet that love asks for something in return, that we make the effort to love one another and to do whatever it takes to remain close to God.

As the months passed and I was still writing this book, I pondered whether this story of Patrick and me, our story of forgiveness and healing, needed to be told. It is a remarkable testament to the power of forgiveness. Yet I was not sure I wanted to end the story with this bombshell. I would describe the relationship between us as partners on a divine healing journey. What was my hesitation about? As I was getting close to completing my story, I still had not shared my ongoing correspondence with Patrick with anyone but a handful of people. I simply had never figured out how to reveal this miraculous and unbelievable story. Eventually the answer seemed to come out of the blue one day, but I knew better—that Spirit was working through me again!

It should be a part of your book, of your entire faith journey.

I could only shake my head in wonder, as I now understood why I had to get to this time and this place in my continuing life story to complete my book. All those years ago, I had questioned God as to why I had been given another chance to live but Dana had had to die, as to why I was left here, and what God wanted from me. This God I believe in had answered my questions in a most inconceivable, astonishing manner. He had chosen me to accomplish His work, to help Patrick Ford heal from and forgive himself for murdering my daughter! With that revelation, I was now convinced this mission—a mission of forgiveness, of mercy, of healing, and of rebirth—was what I had been moving toward all along, and the result is the divine journey both Patrick and I have been sharing. Also, I strongly feel Dana has played a role in this spiritual journey; she has been my guardian angel and my advocate along the way. Deep in my heart, I believe she knew this is what I needed for myself. And, I am convinced this is what she would have wanted for me and for Patrick. Even as I write this, I cannot fathom why I was chosen for this journey and frequently have been brought to tears with the miracle and mystery of it all. But I am in awe of God's work done through me and am humbled to have been chosen by Him to tell my story.

This is my incredible, Spirit-guided faith journey. Given the deep pain and sorrow I had held in my heart after my daughter was murdered, it was quite a revelation that only by the grace of God had I been able to forgive her murderer. To this day, over nine years ago now since Dana's death, I am still in awe of that grace given to me to forgive Patrick Ford. Forgiving him is so much more of a miracle knowing, even now, I find myself having difficulty forgiving others whose perceived transgressions against me are so inconsequential in comparison. And then I remind myself that, as a flawed human being, I will continue to struggle every day of my life, needing to forgive and be forgiven. But my powerful spiritual awakening will always remind me that reconciliation brings me the power of God's healing, freedom, lightness, and peace.

CHAPTER 32

COMING FULL CIRCLE

The wound is the place where the Light enters you.
— Jalaluddin Rumi

I am now living my new normal. I am living a full life, working part time in the travel industry, exploring the world whenever the opportunity presents itself, enjoying my many hobbies, volunteering, and spending precious time with Joe and Sarah, my seven siblings and their families, and Joe's family, whenever possible. I have an amazing group of "sister friends" who have shared this incredible journey with me, gifting me with their love, friendship, and unwavering support through it all. I value the relationship I have with each one of these women. I treasure our time together, whether it has been sharing a meal; watching a movie together; hiking, biking, or cruising with them in this country or abroad; enjoying a girls' getaway weekend; sitting quietly while reading and savoring a wonderful hot cup of coffee; or simply talking and laughing for hours on end. I am richly blessed to have this group of women friends.

My spiritual life is my rock and my fortress, and my spiritual advisor, Father Joji, is a special friend. God is at the center of my life, my guiding force. I have learned to listen, ponder, pray, and act with the Spirit as my guide. And I have come to fully trust in this relationship with my God.

What a refreshing reversal this has been. I am in awe of how easy it is for me most of the time now to recognize when I am troubled, how natural it has become for me to humbly ask the Spirit for guidance, and how trustingly I can accept that an answer will be revealed when I am ready to proceed. These answers have come to me in so many ways: from that little voice in my head; my daily prayer and reflection time; a favorite Bible verse; a conversation with a friend, family member, my spiritual advisor, or even a stranger; the priest's homily (or sermon) shared with us at Mass; or reading a book or a magazine article. The most important thing for me, always, is to keep an open heart and an open mind as to how the Spirit is trying to speak to me. What I do with the answer is always for me to decide.

I pray often in thanksgiving and in gratitude for all God continues to bless me with. My daily prayer has become "You are my light and my life. You are my salvation, of whom should I fear? You are my life's refuge, of whom should I be afraid?" (paraphrased from Psalm 27:1), "Christ be my light, shine in my heart, shine through my darkness" (paraphrased from song "Christ, Be Our Light" by Bernadette Farrell and Frank Brownstead). What I have come to believe with every fiber of my being is that we as individuals each have our own light to bring to the world, and we must let our light shine to bring more love to each other and to our broken world. I pray I may be a light to all those who have been a light for me in my utter darkness, and that I may walk with them throughout their life journeys. I will always struggle to do the right thing. And I am certain there will be times in which I fail. But I have complete confidence that I will never be alone as I struggle and as I respectfully try to be a light to those with whom I come in contact, to do my small part to make a difference in our world.

Each of our lives is fluid, ever changing, and unpredictable. My life story, as well as each of yours, continues as every single day holds the potential for a new challenge, a new discovery, a new joy, a new sorrow, a new hardship, a new love. I have suffered so much mentally, physically, and emotionally throughout my life and have experienced unbearable pain at times. I have walked through the fires, letting myself feel the pain and sorrow, and have not only survived but thrived as well as healed in such a miraculous manner. Losing Dana the way we did brought the most immeasurable, unrelenting pain of all, the kind of pain I had never endured before, the kind of pain I could not imagine surviving. That is why, when Dana was murdered, I had trustingly put myself in the loving and comforting arms of God and had prayed incessantly in my total brokenness. Miraculously, I was somehow able to let go of any control I thought I possessed and give myself up to God, because I could not find my way out of the abyss alone. Little did I know that in doing so, I would fully experience God's presence in so many astounding ways—as I slowly healed from the loss of my loving younger daughter, as I let go of all the years of built-up resentment in my marriage and came to a place of contentment, and as I was led along an incredible spiritual journey I could never have imagined in my wildest dreams.

As you know, shortly after Dana's murder, I had no doubt that for me to survive that unimaginable tragedy and heal, I needed to talk about Dana and keep her memory alive. My heart is overflowing with gratitude and love for all the ways in which, collectively, Dana's friends and family have risen to the occasion. Everyone who has donated to our causes in Dana's memory throughout the last nine years has helped all of us who love her to keep her memory shining.

Shortly after our visit to Minneapolis to clean out Dana's apartment, our family had established a scholarship fund in Dana's memory. Our wish at the time had been to create a lasting tribute to Dana that would honor her and, at the same time, contribute to another promising veterinary student's journey. In April 2008, the first recipient of the Dana E. Mangi Memorial Scholarship Fund was a young woman from Dana's class. As of mid-2009, the memorial scholarship fund had become the Dana E. Mangi Memorial Endowment Fund when the amount reached a balance of over $25,000! The first endowment scholarship was given out in the spring of 2011, and yearly scholarships will be awarded to honor Dana's spirit into perpetuity.

Our family was invited to the University of Minnesota College of Veterinary Medicine Commencement 2011 ceremony for Dana's graduating class. The officials from the university posthumously awarded Dana and our family her doctor of veterinary medicine degree. Sarah and I accepted the award on Dana's behalf that evening. As difficult and bittersweet as it was, I cherished the opportunity to stand with Dana's classmates and honor their accomplishments. Even though she had not met most of those who would have been her classmates, she had been working at the veterinary college pharmacy during the summer of 2007 and had befriended some of her classmates then. I had been told Dana was considered part of this tight-knit group of students in the graduating class of 2011.

"Just her memory and her honor is something they all feel like they're carrying forward," said Bill Venne, the chief development officer for the veterinary college.

What an amazing tribute to my daughter's once-promising life and to her beautiful spirit. I was not able to attend the annual spring awards reception for the College of Veterinary Medicine in 2012. When I received the booklet of all the awards given out that night, I was stunned and teary eyed as I noticed the scholarship was now called the Dr. Dana E. Mangi Memorial Scholarship. As of February 2016, the scholarship fund balance is $46,400!

In July 2016, our PAWS (Pets Are Worth Saving) team, the Mooseketeers, completed our tenth annual walk to raise money for Dana's love of animals. To date, our team has raised just over $33,000. Dana's memory is alive and well at the PAWS Chicago facility. Keeping with our theme of helping animals, the Chicago Anti-Cruelty Society is an organization that helps with the adoption of lost and unwanted animals, as well as offering them medical care. Because we raised so much money for this deserving organization in Dana's honor—to date, about $10,650—we were able to sponsor a commemorative plaque in loving memory. The plaque has been displayed in a planter in their beautiful, welcoming courtyard.

Many generous donations in Dana's memory come into these and other wonderful organizations that help animals and people. Susan G. Komen, formerly known as the Susan G. Komen Breast Cancer Foundation, is a nonprofit organization dedicated to saving lives and ending breast cancer forever. As finding a cure for breast cancer is so important to our family, in lieu of flowers, in Dana's obituary we requested donations to be made to this organization or to the Anti-Cruelty Society of Chicago. To date, about $4,820 has been donated to Susan G. Komen in Dana's memory.

In addition, there are several unique ways in which Dana will live on in our hearts. A group of Dana's friends purchased two commemorative paver bricks at Wrigley Field, the baseball field of Dana's beloved Chicago Cubs, with an inscription reading, "For Dana Mangi, our angel in the outfield." One brick is a memento for our family, and the other is embedded with other commemorative pavers in the sidewalk entering Wrigley Field. Our family sponsored a memorial brick in the courtyard garden of our church as well as a bench in Dana's memory on the grounds of Midwestern University, where she had graduated with her master's degree in biomedical sciences in the spring of 2007. An inscription on the bench reads, "In loving memory of Dana Elizabeth Mangi . . . Your friends at Midwestern University." And, most recently, Joe, Sarah, and I were so touched and honored when one of Dana's closest girlfriends named her newborn baby girl Dana Rose, in memory of her friend and of our daughter. I am in awe with all we, collectively, have accomplished in Dana's memory.

I recently found a card I had written to Dana on December 31, 2006. At the time, she was still in a state of flux in her life's journey, waiting to see if she would be accepted into any veterinary school or medical school within the next few months. No matter where she might be accepted, she would be separating from us, starting a new beginning in her life's calling. In the card, I shared with her that it was the feast of the Holy Family (Jesus, Mary, and Joseph), December 31, and that a reflection from our church bulletin had touched me as her mother. Then I included a part of the reflection: "Our children are all gifts from the Lord. They have been borrowed to us for a short time. They belong to God and we have been allowed the great privilege to grow-them-up [sic] for the One who made them. In the gospel, we hear the story of Jesus separating himself from his parents so that he could be about his life's calling." I ended the note telling Dana I was so proud of who she was, of how she was going about her life's calling, and that my hope was that 2007 would bring her a clearer picture of what that path would be. When I found this treasure, reading it took my breath away for several different reasons. It was with incredible melancholy I now knew our borrowed time had ended less than nine months later. It was also with such joy that I had not missed an opportunity, because life is so precious and temporary, to share with Dana how much I loved her and how proud I was of her.

The reflection itself reinforced my belief that Dana had been our gift from God for her short time on this earth, that she had been called back to the One who had made her. There will always be times when I am struck unaware of the loss of Dana in my life and in my family. That is a part of my life now. But, in my Catholic Christian faith, I believe God's kingdom will have no end, and I pray that one day I will enjoy a life in God's eternal, heavenly kingdom. Honestly, most often when I imagine Dana, I have this beautiful picture in my head of her flitting around her heavenly home like Tinkerbell from *Peter Pan*, doing her thing, full of peace, love, joy, and taking her job of my advocate and my guardian angel seriously. Dana will always be in my heart and in my soul. I hope to one day be united with my God and Father and to be reunited with my Dana as well as with all my loved ones who have gone before me.

After I could let go of my resentment toward my husband for shutting me out of his world after Dana died, the weight of my impossible expectations had been lifted at the end of 2008. I was emotionally healthy enough at that time to finally accept Joe for where he was in his healing journey and to admit we all need to grieve in our own way and in our own time. Even so, at times I still was unhappy that we could not share in our loss. As time passed, though, I became increasingly successful at letting go of my judgment when I felt an emotional disconnect with Joe. Instead of that immediate resentment and anger, my focus was on reminding myself that we each needed to take care of ourselves in our healing journeys.

It is ironic that I was often disgusted with how long the court process had dragged on, but in hindsight, those two and a half years had been essential to my continued emotional healing. I had needed that amount of time to heal in such a way as to accept the sincerity of Patrick's words to us at the plea-agreement hearing, to recognize that I needed to decompress from the grueling court process, and then to live life to the fullest. I also believe that the gift of time was essential for me to soften my heart and put into perspective how sorry I was that Joe and I had not been able to share our unbearable heartbreak. It was with immense sorrow that I realized how much more each of us had suffered because of our inability to support each other.

Rediscovering common interests, having fun together as a couple, and just living again in our new normal has brought me a renewed commitment to be open and honest in my marriage. Joe and I have made a life together for over forty-two years. We have raised two most amazing young women whom we will forever love with all our hearts. We have weathered possibly the worst storm we will ever face together. The percentage of couples who stay together after losing a child is extremely low, but by the grace of God, we have beat the odds. I can only speak for myself, but I am more content in my marriage than I have been for many years.

My relationship with my daughter, Sarah, is stronger and deeper than ever. Sarah and I have lovingly and respectfully supported each other's journey of healing after Dana's death. Without her unconditional love for me as well as her ability to open herself willingly to feel our shared sorrow and pain, even as painful as that was, I do not know if I could have survived Dana's murder. We have both grown so much because of this journey we were forced to take, and I am thankful I can now be transparent with Sarah in sharing my journey with Patrick.

I believe Sarah and I are kindred spirits in so many ways. I witness every day this most beautiful young woman, whose spirit has been wounded many times and crushed with Dana's death, continuing to live life and meet her every challenge head on. We share a love of deep conversations and lively discussions about many topics in the world around us. It is during these times—when I experience her keen intellect, her great sense of curiosity, her faith in God, and her positive outlook—that I am energized and reminded of a favorite quote of mine, my motto for living now: "Surround yourself only with people who fill you up. Get rid of the toxic ones" (Hoda Kotb). Sarah's inner beauty and inner light shine as I observe her strength in adversity, her ability to love with all of her heart, her compassion, and her loyalty for those she cares deeply about. I love Sarah more than my own life. I am extremely honored that I can be a part of her continuing life journey, and I am so proud to call her my daughter.

Throughout those years after Dana died, I was moving along a path that, unbeknownst to me, would open my hardened heart toward Patrick Ford. This extraordinary change of heart not only allowed me to forgive this young man, but also brought about such a wondrous series of events that would change me forever. Not only had I agreed to receive that first letter from Patrick, but our correspondence has continued now for over two years, helping me to grow in my spiritual and emotional life as well as get to know Patrick as a person, not just as my daughter's murderer. Miraculously, I have come to care about this young man as he has shared his deepest, flawed self with me, his fears, his self-doubts, his sorrows, his daily struggles, and his continued path toward healing. In witnessing this transformation of both Patrick and myself—emotionally, mentally, and spiritually—I have realized I am more at peace than I have been in a long time.

Patrick asked me numerous times throughout our correspondences how I was doing and if I would be willing to explain how I had been able to heal. Even though I attempted to describe my healing journey in more depth each time he asked me that question, I never seemed to be successful in assuaging his self-inflicted prison of guilt and remorse. So at some point, I decided I wanted to send him a copy of this story if it were ever completed. In my heart, I felt this would be the best way for him or anyone else to understand how I was able to get to where I am today. We had talked about my book in the context of my healing journey and how much of it was related to our story, his and mine. He had expressed an interest in reading the book and also had given me permission to use his written words.

Although I had totally discounted the idea of ever visiting Patrick, in one of our conversations Father Joji shared that if I ever did want to visit Patrick, he would accompany me. Nothing more was decided that day other than that I told him I was happy to know he would be there with me. However, I still could not imagine that scenario. At the time, I continued to believe I had found true healing in the spiritual connection Patrick and I shared in our letter writing. I was happy with that reality; it seemed enough for me until, yet again, an unexpected thought whirling around in my head nagged at me. What was it this time? Trust me, I did not sit around waiting for these thoughts or words to enter my brain. They just popped into my head at the most unexpected times!

What about visiting Patrick at some point? Then you can just bring him a copy of the book.

I sat with that thought for some time, and although I had come to no resolution, I was softening as I thought about the what-ifs of visiting Patrick. Then, one morning in early 2016 as I was having breakfast with my girlfriend, Timi, I confided in her. She asked me if I had ever thought about what I would say or do if I did visit him. Would I go in there, ask him how he was doing and what had been going on in his life, like you might do with a friend? My immediate reaction was "Oh God, NO! That is not the kind of relationship I have with Patrick!" Timi's question gave me pause, though. What I did come to realize from our conversation was that I definitely wanted to deliver this book to Patrick. What I did not yet understand was why that was so important to me. And what would I do or say when I got there?

After some reflection, I concluded that I needed to just let go of my building anxiety and doubts, and at some later time when I was ready, the answer would reveal itself to me.

Our leader in the Roman Catholic Church, Pope Francis, had designated the year of 2016 as the Year of Mercy, beginning on December 8, 2015, and ending on November 20, 2016. Pope Francis had called upon all Catholics to be witnesses to mercy and to "find the joy of rediscovering and rendering fruitful God's mercy, with which we are all called to give comfort to every man and every woman of our time," as well as to live by the words of Jesus: "Be merciful, even as your Father is merciful" (Luke 6:36). I was touched by Pope Francis's words. I began to understand that what he was asking of us was what I was being called to do, to show mercy toward Patrick and to finally meet this young man whom I have come to care about, face to face. This revelation answered the question of why I was drawn to visiting him at this time—to show mercy and to forgive him in person. For once I had no hesitation about the message. I was sure this was what I wanted to do; the idea of seeing Patrick and talking to him seemed right to me. And although the thought of visiting Patrick for the first time terrified me, it also enlightened me as to where the path was leading me. This seemed like the perfect time to meet with Father Joji once again.

When we next met, Father Joji and I talked about the Year of Mercy and how I had been so moved by the pope's message. Having a dialogue with Father Joji about all my angst associated with the first prison visit brought me a sense of calmness and peace. He reminded me it was not necessary to plan what I would do and say when I visited Patrick if I simply let the Spirit guide my way. Because I could not imagine how I would act upon meeting Patrick in person, I had felt such a sense of relief during our discussion when I realized I had no interest whatsoever in orchestrating that first prison meeting. One thing was certain, though: I had been convinced for quite some time that the Spirit had shepherded me so far in the development of this spiritual relationship I have with Patrick. Thus, I did not hesitate to put my trust in the Spirit to work with me and through me in this endeavor, whenever it would happen.

Father Joji was such a wonderful example of Pope Francis's call to be a witness to mercy that afternoon by being there for me, by being an attentive listener, and by talking through all of the issues I had brought to the discussion. I am blessed and grateful for the gift of Father Joji in my life.

Recently, as I was still struggling with the ending to my book, I happened to be reading an article about forgiveness and reconciliation called "Forgiveness," written by Barbara Mahany. The article gave me such a clear understanding of the distinction between forgiveness and reconciliation. Forgiving Patrick Ford was a private spiritual act I believe I was only able to accomplish with God's grace, and only after several years of prayer and meditation after Dana's death. That was my choice alone to forgive Patrick. But forgiveness and reconciliation are two completely different things. Reconciliation involves at least one other person, and both people must be willing to do what it takes to heal the relationship.

After reading that article, I was stunned when I realized the immensity of all that was drawing me to visit Patrick. What I had never considered at all, until I reflected on that article, was that it was Patrick who was willing to take the first step in our reconciliation story when he had spoken at the plea-agreement hearing. His words had opened my heart to feel compassion and sadness for him that day, and soon after, I knew I forgave him. That was when my life changed forever, and that was when the seed of reconciliation between us was planted. Then again, in July 2014, he persisted when he courageously wrote his first letter to me. He had reached out to me in reconciliation twice before I felt safe enough to take my own step. So, as I pondered that definition of reconciliation, I concluded that we had both been doing our part to create a most improbable, unbelievable personal relationship born out of a gaping wound, a wound so deep one would think it would have been impossible to ever heal. And yet, miraculously we could heal it together, each in our own ways. Not only is our story a remarkable testament to the power of forgiveness, but it is also a miraculous, amazing story of reconciliation!

In Patrick's first letter to my sister, Tina, back in early 2014, he had written that he desperately wanted to apologize in person because he hurt so badly for all of us and wanted to help any way he could. He said that even if someone just wanted to scream at him or spit in his face, he would be okay with that if it helped someone. When Tina read that to me back then, we were still skeptical and questioning whether his letter and his words were too good to be true. Obviously, I was not ready to even entertain the idea of going to the prison and meeting him face to face. But during our years of correspondence, as I got to know this young man in a deeply personal way, to build a trusting relationship with him through our letters, and to appreciate all of the things he had done and continued to do to improve his emotional and spiritual self, I could acknowledge that Patrick is much more than the crime he committed against Dana and all who love her. This was our astounding reconciliation story!

I could only shake my head in gratitude and awe that I had been drawn to that article just as I was struggling with ending the book. What I had already known before reading the article was that I wanted to tell Patrick face to face that I had forgiven him. What I had never felt, until after I reflected on the message in the article, was the intense desire to thank Patrick for planting the seed of our reconciliation story at the plea-agreement hearing. Because of this entire experience, I knew without a doubt it was time to write to Patrick to ask if I could come visit him. With all of that said, how can I ever doubt that the Holy Spirit continues to work through me in so many extraordinary ways?

Assuming that a visit with Patrick was imminent, I finally opened up to Joe about the fact we had been corresponding for over two years and that I would be planning a trip to see Patrick in prison hopefully before the end of 2016. In the spirit of being honest with my husband in our marriage, I wanted to reveal the part of myself I had kept secret for too long, even though I was nervous about what his reaction would be. Without hesitation, Joe acknowledged that he understood I needed to do this for my healing. This was my journey to take. What an incredible feeling of relief washed over me knowing the two people whom I love most now knew me more intimately. And what a testament to where Joe and I have come in our marriage. I thank God for that every day.

Patrick and I have been in communication about setting up our visit, hopefully to take place sometime in 2017. Our visit has been approved, and Patrick has shared with me all the procedures we must follow.

He was moved to another facility in late 2016. Once I learned about the move, I decided to wait until spring before making the long drive to visit him. My book will most likely not be published then, but that gift will come in time. Right now, this visit is what I am being called to do in my heart and in my soul. And I look forward to taking this next step with the Spirit guiding my way. I will just have to wait patiently to see what the future holds regarding the timing of my book's publication and when I will be able to bring a copy to Patrick.

In my ever-evolving personal relationship with God, I believe I was gently led to where I am today. Out of this inconceivable tragedy in my family, something wonderful has happened to me. God's loving guidance can be revealed in wonderful, mysterious, and personal ways. This God of mine has helped me find the way to a new life, to a reawakening of lightness and peace in my soul.

ACKNOWLEDGMENTS

First, I have been blessed to have had the unconditional support and encouragement of my beloved daughter, Sarah Mangi, throughout the entire process of writing my book. Not only did she read sections of the book more than once, she also found time to edit the entire manuscript and offer indispensable feedback that was so valuable for improving the book.

Special thanks go to my friend, Katie Cory, the first person to suggest I write a book about my healing journey. I remember the moment she asked me if I had ever thought about writing a book. Although I had no intention of doing so back then, she planted the seed that day, which was nourished until I was ready and eager to share my story.

Dr. Rita Corley, my psychotherapist for many years, was instrumental in guiding me through the revisions of my early manuscript, as I had grappled with conveying my emotional struggles and what I had learned from them. She has been one of the most influential women in my adult life, and I will always have a special place in my heart for her. She was a special gift from God when I was at one of the lowest points in my life.

I am especially grateful for my early readers who gave their time to read my manuscript (sometimes more than once) and offered me their heartfelt comments and suggestions. To my dearest friends, Timi Demitropoulos, Nancy Olson, and Sally Graham, as well as my sister, Cindy Peters, I am eternally thankful for their help and their longtime friendship.

Thanks also to those few readers who were only given my final version of the manuscript: Barb Brandes, Carol Phillips, Father Matt Foley, Father Joji Thanugundla, and my sister-in-law Linda Mangi-Vogel. These readers supported me with constructive comments and enthusiasm for the book's publication.

For all my family, Joe's family, and my friends who encouraged my writing over the years, I thank them for their patience. I appreciate their anticipation and excitement during these last several years.

I want to give special thanks to Mike Falagario, our prosecutor in the case against Patrick Ford, for reviewing those sections of my book related to the court case. I felt compelled to get his approval that what I said in layman's terms, regarding everything from the arrest to Patrick Ford's plea agreement, was accurate. Mike met with me several times and read through many pages of my manuscript, even though he was busy working and teaching. I cherish his kindness and all his help with my manuscript.

To Paul Maganzini, an attorney and a longtime friend of ours, my deepest gratitude for all his help reviewing each contract between myself and Mountain Arbor Press, for explaining in layman's terms what I did not understand, for answering any questions I had, and for giving me his trusted legal advice to protect my interests in this exciting endeavor of publishing my first book.

To my sister Tina Mercier, for having the courage and the heart to initiate the correspondence with Patrick Ford. She was the catalyst for all that transpired among the three of us. Her first letter charted a course that led me on a miraculous, faith-filled, and life-changing journey.

Finally, and most amazingly, I want to acknowledge my gratitude toward and my profound thanks to Patrick Ford for the courage to speak from his heart to our family at his plea-agreement hearing in March 2010. His words that day changed my life forever, setting me on a course of action I still cannot fully fathom. That course of action, that part of my healing journey, became an integral part of my book and led to a most miraculous, unbelievable ending to my story. I am humbled by and in awe of the miracle and mystery of God choosing me to tell my story.

ADDITIONAL RESOURCES

BOOKS

Amatuzio, Janis. *Forever Ours: Real Stories of Immortality and Living from a Forensic Pathologist.* Novato, CA: New World Library, 2004.

Piper, Don and Cecil Murphey. *90 Minutes in Heaven: A True Story of Death & Life.* Grand Rapids, MI: Baker Publishing Group, 2004.

Sanders, Catherine M. *How to Survive the Loss of a Child: Filling the Emptiness and Rebuilding Your Life.* New York, NY: Three Rivers Press, 1998.

The Dads Group. *Tuesday Mornings with the Dads: Stories by Fathers Who Have Lost a Son or a Daughter.* Forward by Tony Dungy, Portland, OR: Inkwater Press, 2009.

Zonnebelt-Smeenge, Susan J. and Robert C. De Vries. *The Empty Chair: Handling Grief on Holidays and Special Occasions.* Grand Rapids, MI: Baker Book House Company, 2004.

POEMS

"Ascension," Colleen Corah Hitchcock

"Far, but Near," Peggy Werner

"Gone from My Sight," Henry van Dyke

"It's Time," Pam Reinke

"Do Not Stand at My Grave and Weep," Mary Elizabeth Frye

"She Is Gone," David Harkins

"The Elephant in the Room," Terry Kettering

Barbara A. Mangi

FAVORITE SCRIPTURE VERSES

Scripture verses listed are from The New American Bible (Revised Edition), copyright © 2010, 1991, 1986, 1970 Confraternity of Christian Doctrine, Inc., Washington, DC

Isaiah 43:2
2 When you pass through waters, I will be with you;
through rivers, you shall not be swept away.
When you walk through fire, you shall not be burned,
nor will flames consume you.

Psalm 13:3
3 How long must I carry sorrow in my soul,
grief in my heart day after day?
How long will my enemy triumph over me?

Psalm 23:1–4, 6
1 A psalm of David.
I
The LORD is my shepherd;
there is nothing I lack.
2 In green pastures he makes me lie down;
to still waters he leads me;
3 he restores my soul.
He guides me along right paths
for the sake of his name.
4 Even though I walk through the valley of the shadow of death,
I will fear no evil, for you are with me;
your rod and your staff comfort me.
II
6 Indeed, goodness and mercy will pursue me
all the days of my life;
I will dwell in the house of the LORD
for endless days.

Psalm 30:3, 12–13

³ O LORD, my God,
I cried out to you for help and you healed me.
¹² You changed my mourning into dancing;
you took off my sackcloth
and clothed me with gladness.
¹³ So that my glory may praise you
and not be silent.
O LORD, my God,
forever will I give you thanks.

Psalm 34:19

¹⁹ The LORD is close to the brokenhearted,
saves those whose spirit is crushed.

Psalm 18:7

⁷ In my distress I called out: LORD!
I cried out to my God.
From his temple he heard my voice;
my cry to him reached his ears.

Jeremiah 29:11–12

¹¹ For I know well the plans I have in mind for you—oracle of the LORD—plans for your welfare and not for woe, so as to give you a future of hope.
¹² When you call me, and come and pray to me, I will listen to you.

Isaiah 40:31

³¹ They that hope in the LORD will renew their strength,
they will soar on eagles' wings;
They will run and not grow weary,
walk and not grow faint.

Psalm 28:7
⁷ The LORD is my strength and my shield,
in whom my heart trusts.
I am helped, so my heart rejoices;
with my song I praise him.

Ezekiel 34:16
¹⁶ The lost I will search out, the strays I will bring back, the injured I will bind up, and the sick I will heal; but the sleek and the strong I will destroy. I will shepherd them in judgment.

Matthew 11:28–30
The Gentle Mastery of Christ.
²⁸ "Come to me, all you who labor and are burdened, and I will give you rest.
²⁹ Take my yoke upon you and learn from me, for I am meek and humble of heart; and you will find rest for yourselves.
³⁰ For my yoke is easy, and my burden light."

Luke 6:36–38
³⁶ Be merciful, just as [also] your Father is merciful.

Judging Others.
³⁷ "Stop judging and you will not be judged. Stop condemning and you will not be condemned. Forgive and you will be forgiven.
³⁸ Give and gifts will be given to you; a good measure, packed together, shaken down, and overflowing, will be poured into your lap. For the measure with which you measure will in return be measured out to you."

Luke 12:24–26
²⁴ Notice the ravens: they do not sow or reap; they have neither storehouse nor barn, yet God feeds them. How much more important are you than birds!
²⁵ Can any of you by worrying add a moment to your life-span?
²⁶ If even the smallest things are beyond your control, why are you anxious about the rest?

Isaiah 58:9–11

⁹ Then you shall call, and the LORD will answer,
you shall cry for help, and he will say: "Here I am!"
If you remove the yoke from among you,
the accusing finger, and malicious speech;
¹⁰ If you lavish your food on the hungry
and satisfy the afflicted;
Then your light shall rise in the darkness,
and your gloom shall become like midday;
¹¹ Then the LORD will guide you always
and satisfy your thirst in parched places,
will give strength to your bones
And you shall be like a watered garden,
like a flowing spring whose waters never fail.

Psalm 92:2, 5

² It is good to give thanks to the LORD,
to sing praise to your name, Most High,

⁵ For you make me jubilant, LORD, by your deeds;
at the works of your hands I shout for joy.

Psalm 103:1–2
Praise of Divine Goodness
¹ Of David.
Bless the LORD, my soul;
all my being, bless his holy name!
² Bless the LORD, my soul;
and do not forget all his gifts,

Ecclesiastes 3:1–2

¹ There is an appointed time for everything,
and a time for every affair under the heavens.
² A time to give birth, and a time to die;
a time to plant, and a time to uproot the plant.

BIBLIOGRAPHY

Fumia, Molly. *Safe Passage: Words to Help the Grieving.* York Beach, ME: Conari Press, 2003.

Lawton, Liam. "In the Quiet." *In the Quiet.* Gia Publications, Inc. 2002.

Mahany, Barbara. *Forgiven.* From the Northwestern University magazine called *Northwestern: For Alumni and Friends of Northwestern University* (Summer 2015).

McLachlan, Sarah. "I Will Remember You." *Mirrorball.* Arista Records, Inc., April 1999.

Stillwell, Elaine E. *The Death of a Child: Reflections for Grieving Parents.* Skokie, IL: ACTA Publications, 2004.

4Him. Harris, Mark R (writer). "Let the Healing Begin." *Walk On.* Universal Music Publishing Group, 2001.

Pope Francis. *The Announcement of the Jubilee of Mercy.* From the website www.iubilaeummisericordiae.va/content/gdm/en/giubileo/annuncio.html. March 13, 2015.

ABOUT THE AUTHOR

Barbara A. Mangi was born and raised in Green Bay, Wisconsin, the second oldest of eight children. She graduated from Wisconsin State University–LaCrosse (now University of Wisconsin–LaCrosse) with a bachelor's degree in mathematics and a minor in computer science. She lives with her husband, Joe, and their little Yorkshire terrier, Gizmo, in Arlington Heights, Illinois. Their daughter, Sarah, recently moved back to the Chicago suburbs from San Francisco, and they are thrilled to have her home again. In addition to writing her first book, Barbara works in the travel industry and thoroughly enjoys the opportunity to work with individual clients to make their travel dreams come true.